# ANCHORED IN THE WORD

## Forty Bible Verses That Shaped My Life

## By
## Kow Abaka Essuman

# ANCHORED IN THE WORD:
## FORTY BIBLE VERSES THAT SHAPED MY LIFE

By
Kow Abaka Essuman

Scripture quotations are taken from various versions of the Holy Bible, namely King James Version, New King James Version, New International Version and New Living Translation.

Published in New York, U.S.A.
Printed in Accra, Ghana
First Edition – November 2025

Library of Congress Control Number: 2025923627
ISBN: 979-8-9985882-0-4
Cover Design: Felix Frimpong
Printed by: Kow Abaka Essuman

# DEDICATION

To the One who called me,
sustained me,
and never let me go.

To Jesus Christ,
my anchor, my Shepherd,
and my greatest reward.

And to my family, friends, and loved ones,
thank you for walking this journey with me,
for your love, your faith, and your prayers.

This book is my gift to you,
a testimony that God's Word is still alive,
still powerful,
and still speaking today.

# AUTHOR'S NOTE

When I first received the instruction to write Anchored in the Word, I had no idea how much it would mean to me, or how quickly it would have to happen. What you are holding is not the result of long planning or perfect timing; it is the result of obedience.

Every verse in this book has a story; some told through tears, others through laughter. They represent moments when I felt God's presence more closely than ever and times when I could only trust that He was near, even in silence.

I hope that as you read through these forty verses and reflections, you will not only see traces of my journey but also find pieces of your own. Perhaps, you will remember the verse that steadied you through loss, or the one that ignited your courage when fear tried to win.

Take your time with this book. Reflect, pray, and listen. The Word of God has a way of speaking differently to each of us, depending on where we are.

I pray that as you turn these pages, you will discover,

too, that His Word never returns empty. It heals, restores, corrects, and anchors.

Thank you for sharing in this journey of faith with me. May these pages remind you that life's truest stability comes when you are anchored in the Word.

**Kow Abaka Essuman**
*Accra, Ghana*
*November 2025*

# ACKNOWLEDGEMENTS

First and foremost, I give thanks to God Almighty, my Source and Sustainer. Every word in this book is a testament to Your grace and faithfulness. You have been my anchor in calm and in storm, and through Your Word, I have found strength, peace, and purpose. Without Your voice, this book would not exist; without Your strength, it could not have been completed. To You alone be all the glory.

To my spiritual mentors and pastors, namely, Most Rev. Prof. Johnson K. Asamoah-Gyadu, Most Rev. Dr. Robert Aboagye-Mensah, the late Very Rev. Emmanuel Archer, Prophet Gideon Danso, and Rev. Dr. Nii Sorse Tackie-Yarboi, thank you for your teachings, prayers, and example. Each of you has played a part in shaping my walk with God and deepening my understanding of His Word.

To my beautiful wife, Lady-Ann, thank you for walking beside me with grace, patience, and unwavering love. You have been my partner in every sense, my confidant, prayer warrior, and greatest earthly gift. You embody Proverbs 31 in every way.

To our children, Papa Kwesi Abaka and Ewuradwoa

Okyerewa Krofa, you are daily reminders of God's goodness. May you grow anchored in the Word, guided by truth, and driven by purpose. Watching you grow has been one of life's greatest joys.

To my father, Professor Ato Essuman, and my mother, Professor Salome Essuman, thank you for raising me on a foundation of faith, discipline, and love. You were my first teachers of integrity, humility, and service, and everything I am today rests on the values you instilled in me.

To my brothers, Nana Kow Appiah Essuman, Dr. Kow Mensah Akaa Essuman, and Nana Yaw Atiapa Essuman, thank you for being my lifelong companions, cheerleaders, and friends. Your encouragement and quiet strength have been constant sources of support and joy.

To my boss and mentor, the former President of Ghana, Nana Addo Dankwa Akufo-Addo, thank you for your love, guidance, and the countless lessons learned from serving you over the years. Your wisdom, courage, and example have left an indelible mark on my life. To Mrs. Rebecca Akufo-Addo, whom I consider a mother, thank you for your affection, encouragement, and kindness from the very first day we met.

To Vice President Dr. Mahamudu Bawumia and Hajia Samira Bawumia, thank you for your friendship and encouragement. It has been a privilege to know and learn from both of you.

To Hon. Akosua Frema Osei Opare, thank you for trusting me, empowering me, and giving me opportunities to serve and excel. To Ambassador Nana Bediatuo Asante, thank you for believing in me even when I doubted myself. You gave me room to grow and the confidence to lead. To Madam Saratu Atta, thank you for being another mother to me, nurturing me with love and always looking out for my physical and spiritual well-being. To Gabby Asare Otchere-Darko, thank you for seeing in me what I did not see many years ago and for your constant encouragement to remain focused and assertive. Your push and support in many ways have made an impact in my life.

To the late Kojo Bentsi-Enchill, thank you for your mentorship and wisdom during my time at Cornell Law School and beyond. You believed in me, challenged me to be excellent, and taught me that success means little without character. To Ace Anan Ankomah, thank you for pushing me to return home and pursue purpose over comfort. Your confidence in me, your counsel, and your concern for my well-being have meant more than words can express.

To all my friends, colleagues, and loved ones who have supported me on this journey, thank you for your prayers, encouragement, and love. Many of you have lived through the stories behind these verses and witnessed firsthand how God's Word has worked in my life. Your support has been God's grace expressed through human hearts.

To those who helped bring this project to life, editors, designers, and those who simply reminded me to keep writing, thank you. This book was written in obedience but made possible through your encouragement.

Finally, to everyone who will read Anchored in the Word, thank you for letting me share my journey with you. I pray that as you turn these pages, the same Word that shaped my life will speak to yours, bringing strength, peace, and direction for your own walk of faith.

This book is my offering of gratitude, to God, to my family, and to everyone who has poured into my life.

May it bless you as your lives have blessed mine.

To God be the glory; great things He has done, and greater things He will yet do.

# TABLE OF CONTENTS

# INTRODUCTION

One of my desires before my fortieth birthday was to publish a book. It had long been my desire to do so. I imagined a reflective memoir titled *The First Forty*, a recount of my journey so far, the lessons learned, the milestones reached, and the faith and favour that sustained me. It was an ambitious project; one I began with great enthusiasm. But along the way, another manuscript, a more urgent and weighty work titled *Governance and the Law in Ghana*, demanded my attention. That project, which is still underway, took centre stage, and *The First Forty* had to be shelved.

As my fortieth birthday drew near, I felt a strong stirring in my spirit; a yearning to pause, reflect, and express gratitude. I decided to embark on a forty-day fast: forty days to thank God for forty years of His grace, favour, and protection and to seek His direction for the years ahead. It was not a fast of routine or ritual but one of reverence, a time to look back at the path behind me and forward to the journey still unfolding.

Near the end of that fast, during one of my midnight prayer sessions, I heard a quiet but unmistakable instruction in my spirit: *"Write a book about forty Bible verses that have influenced your life."*

It wasn't an idea I had planned or even considered. But I have learned that when God gives an instruction, obedience is the only appropriate response. You may not understand the timing, the reason, or even the full picture, but once the word is spoken, your duty is simply to follow.

The timing, however, could not have been more demanding; I had only ten days until my fortieth birthday. Yet, the conviction in my heart was so clear that I could not ignore it. After that midnight prayer, I sat down and began to list the forty verses that had shaped my life, verses that had guided my decisions, comforted me in sorrow, lifted me in uncertainty, and anchored my faith through every storm.

That list became the foundation of this book.

Each of these forty verses represents a chapter in my life's story, not just the story of my faith but God's faithfulness. They are scriptures that have spoken to me in moments of triumph and in times of trial; words that have corrected me, comforted me, and called me deeper into trust.

For instance, **Matthew 6:33** taught me early on to seek God first and trust Him to take care of the rest.

**Romans 8:28** reminded me, especially in seasons of disappointment, that all things, even those I didn't understand, were working together for my good. **Proverbs 3:5–6** taught me to lean not on my own understanding but to let God direct my path. **Hebrews 12:1–2** reminded me to run my race with endurance, and **Jeremiah 29:11** assured me that God's plans are always better than mine.

These verses, along with many others like them, became the pillars upon which my faith has stood.

This book was not born from ambition but from obedience. It began as an act of gratitude, my way of saying "*thank You*" to God for forty years of unmerited grace, protection, and mercy. My intention was simple: to document these verses and reflections as a keepsake, something I could share with my family, friends, and anyone who chose to celebrate this milestone with me.

But as the words began to flow, I realised this was not just a personal reflection, but a testimony meant to be shared more widely. Perhaps someone, somewhere, is walking through a season that one of these verses carried me through. Perhaps this book would remind them that God's Word still speaks, still guides, still anchors us when the waves of life rise high.

**Anchored in the Word**

The title Anchored in the Word came naturally. Over the years, I have found that no matter where life takes you, in success or challenges, in clarity or confusion, the Word of God steadies you. The storms will come, the winds will blow, but those who are anchored in the Word will not be moved.

This book is, therefore, both a reflection on how the Word has shaped me and an invitation to discover the same power for yourself.

I wrote it under pressure, yes, but also under grace. And as always, God proved that when He calls you to something, He provides everything you need to complete it.

So here it is, a collection of forty verses that have shaped my walk with God, and the lessons, reflections, and revelations that have come from living them out. My prayer is that as you read, you too will find your anchor in His Word.

*"The grass withers and the flowers fade, but the word of our God stands forever."* — **Isaiah 40:8**

# VERSE 1
# MATTHEW 6:33

*But seek ye first the kingdom of God, and his righteousness; and all these things shall be added unto you.*

Every journey of faith begins with a reordering of priorities. There are moments when God gently interrupts our plans to remind us that He must come first. This verse, **Matthew 6:33**, marked one such turning point in my life. It was the moment I began to truly understand what it meant to build my life around God's will and to trust that everything else would fall into place when He was at the centre.

I had read this verse countless times before, but for years, it sat in my mind as a beautiful line of Scripture rather than a personal revelation. It wasn't until early January 2016, a significant moment in my spiritual journey, that the verse truly came alive.

At the time, I was at a crossroads. My life was full of activity and ambition, but I longed for divine direction. I felt a deep stirring to step away from the noise and seek God in solitude. So, I packed a small bag, downloaded a few sermons on YouTube, and drove to Sogakope, to a serene spa and resort called Holy Trinity, a place as peaceful as its name suggested.

It was not meant to be a retreat about luxury; it was about clarity. I had decided that one of my key prayers would be about finding a life partner. It felt like a practical, even necessary, concern for a young man thinking about the next chapter of his life. Yet, as I knelt in prayer and poured my heart out before God, something unexpected happened.

In the stillness, I sensed a quiet but unmistakable voice within me: "*Stop praying about all those things. Seek Me first, and all the others will be added unto you.*"

I paused, almost startled. I knew that voice. It wasn't mine. It was a gentle reminder from my Father in Heaven. I quickly opened my Bible, searched for the verse, and there it was, **Matthew 6:33.** That moment brought me to a realisation. I had been praying about things, not God.

This verse comes at the end of Jesus' teaching on worry, on how we often chase after the wrong priorities: money, possessions, stability, recognition. Jesus pointed to the birds of the air and the lilies of the field, how they neither toil nor spin, yet are cared for by a loving Father. Then He asked, "*Are you not of more value than they?*"

That question struck me deeply. Here I was, anxious about my future, when God had already promised provision if I would simply reorder my priorities: seek His kingdom and His righteousness first.

It's important to note that Jesus did not just say, "*Seek the kingdom of God.*" He added, "a*nd His righteousness.*" The two are inseparable. Seeking God's kingdom means aligning our lives with His rule and purpose, living as His representative on earth. But seeking His righteousness means allowing His nature, His character, to be formed in us. It is a daily walk of integrity, humility, compassion, and obedience.

I have come to learn that when we genuinely seek God first, the things we once chased after begin to chase after us. Opportunities align, peace abounds, and provision finds its way into our lives; not because we schemed or hustled harder, but because we prioritised the right pursuit.

Looking back, I can say without hesitation that every major blessing I've experienced since that retreat, including career breakthroughs, divine relationships, open doors, and peace of mind, has flowed from this simple but profound principle: put God first.

The kingdom of God isn't a distant concept; it's a daily decision to make God the centre of everything – our thoughts, our work, our relationships, our ambitions. When we do that, we discover that what we thought we needed to chase is already waiting for us in His perfect order.

**Prayer**

**Heavenly Father, teach me to seek You above all else. Help me to desire Your kingdom more than success, and Your righteousness more than comfort. Reorder my heart to trust that when I put You first, everything I truly need will follow in Your time. Draw me closer to You each day and let my life be a living testimony of Your faithfulness. In Jesus' name, Amen.**

# VERSE 2
# ROMANS 8:28

*And we know that all things work together for good to them that love God, to them who are the called according to his purpose.*

There are some verses that you read once and move on, and there are others that follow you through life. For me, **Romans 8:28** has always been one of those verses that lingers, like a familiar melody that comes back at just the right moments. I don't even remember when I first discovered it, but I do remember one particular morning when I was meditating on it, and it stayed with me all day. The words carried such quiet strength that I found myself repeating them under my breath: *"And we know that all things work together for good..."*

What strikes me first is how the verse begins with certainty. *"And we know."* Not we think, not we hope, but we know. It's a statement of faith anchored in the character of God. There's a confidence in that declaration, a confidence that no matter what the day holds, no matter what life brings, God is working something out for our good.

Then comes the phrase that always grips me: *"All things."* All things means all things. Not some things. Not only the good things, or the answered prayers, or the joyful moments. All things. The heartbreaks, the disappointments, the betrayals, the failures, the closed doors – all of them somehow find their way into the grand design of God's purpose. When I think back on certain painful seasons in my life, I realise that even in those moments, God was weaving something redemptive, something good, even though I couldn't see it at the time.

But the promise isn't for everyone. Paul makes it clear, it is *"to them that love God, to them who are the called according to His purpose."* That's where the verse turns personal. It invites me to ask myself: *Do I truly love God?*

I once thought about what it really means to love God, and the image that came to mind was that of being in love for the first time. You can't stop thinking about the person. You want to talk to them constantly. You wait eagerly for their message, and your heart leaps when their name appears on your phone. That's how we should be with God. Loving Him means longing to be in His presence, talking to Him often, listening to His voice, delighting in His Word. Prayer becomes less of a duty and more of a conversation. Scripture becomes more than words—it becomes His voice.

Then there's the part about being *"called according to His purpose."* That phrase reminds me that there is a group of people God calls *"the called"*, those who are living in alignment with His divine purpose. When we discover what God has called us to do, and we walk faithfully in it, everything that happens, whether success or setback, serves that purpose. Nothing is wasted in God's plan.

I often find comfort in a hymn from the Methodist Hymn Book, number 511. The final stanza says:

*"Since all that I meet shall work for my good,*
*The bitter is sweet, the medicine food;*
*Though painful at present, 'twill cease before long;*
*And then, O how pleasant the conqueror's song!"*

Those words come alive whenever I face difficult times. They remind me that even the bitter things can be turned sweet in God's hands. Sometimes the pain becomes the medicine we didn't know we needed.

Sometimes the disappointment becomes the door to something better. And often, in hindsight, we see how the puzzle pieces fit perfectly together.

So, if you're going through something right now – uncertainty, loss, or heartbreak – remember this: God is not finished yet. You may not see the full picture now, but one day you will look back and realise that all things really did work together for your good.

**Prayer**

**Heavenly Father, thank You for the assurance of Your Word that all things, every joy and every pain, are working together for my good. Help me to love You deeply, to seek You constantly, and to trust You even when I cannot see the full picture. Teach me to rest in the confidence that You are in control and that nothing in my life is wasted in Your hands. Let every experience draw me closer to You and align me more fully with Your purpose. In Jesus' name, Amen.**

# VERSE 3
# PROVERBS 3:5-6

*Trust in the Lord with all your heart, and lean not on your own understanding; In all your ways acknowledge Him, and He shall direct your paths.*

Trusting God with all our heart is one of the hardest things to do as human beings. It sounds simple, but when life gets complicated, when deadlines are tight, when plans don't go the way we envisioned, or when the path ahead seems uncertain, that's when the real test of trust begins. Most times, we trust God, but not fully. We trust Him with one hand, while holding tightly to our own logic, experience, or plan with the other. We tell ourselves, "*Let me just figure this part out,*" or "*Maybe God needs a little help.*" But this verse invites us to something deeper; to trust Him with all our heart, leaving no room for half-measures or back-up plans.

It's interesting that the verse goes on to say, "*lean not on your own understanding.*" That means even when something seems perfectly logical to us, even when our reasoning or experience suggests a certain path, we are called to pause and seek God's direction. Our understanding, no matter how sharp, is limited. It can fail us, and sometimes, it fails us badly. But God's understanding is infinite. He sees what we cannot see. He knows the turns before we reach them, the storms before they come, and the destination long before we take the first step.

The verse continues: "*In all your ways acknowledge Him.*" That's the key. Acknowledging God means bringing Him into every part of our lives: our plans, our decisions, our relationships, our ambitions, even our pain. It's saying, "*Lord, I can't do this on my own. I need You here.*" When we do that sincerely, Scripture gives us a promise: *He shall direct your paths.*

I've often been asked how I got to where I am today or how certain doors opened in my life. My answer has always been the same: "*It's by the grace of God.*" And I mean it. I've had people laugh at that response or suggest that I rely too much on God, that my achievements were the result of hard work, strategy, or timing, not divine help. But I know deep within that it was never just me, and not only do I know, but I also acknowledge it. God has been my guide, my compass, my direction, and my sustainer. The times I've leaned on my own understanding, I've stumbled.

The times I've trusted Him completely, He's made the way straight.

After serving at the Presidency, I honestly did not know what would become of me or what I was going to do next in my career. It was a strange but peaceful season of uncertainty. Many people asked me, *"So, what's next?"* – and I never had a concrete answer. Often, I would simply respond, *"I'll wait and see what the Lord will do."* Every time I said that, I had this verse, *"Trust in the Lord with all your heart..."*, at the back of my mind. I still don't have everything figured out, even now after turning forty. Yet I don't struggle with that. I've come to a place of quiet confidence, knowing that God will show me what to do next. He has done it before, in fact, many times, and I have no doubt that He will do it again. One of the greatest lessons I've learnt from trusting God is that when you walk with Him, you are not subject to the direction or expectations of people who do not know the end from the beginning. Even if they have walked a similar path before, your story will not end like theirs. Only God knows your end from your beginning, and that's why I choose to trust His direction over anyone else's.

One of my favourite hymns from the Methodist Hymn Book is Hymn number 608, and the final stanza, which reads as follows, serves as a reminder that God directs my path:

*"By Thy unerring spirit led,*
*We shall not in the desert stray,*
*We shall not full direction need,*
*Nor miss our providential way;*
*As far from danger as from dear,*
*While love almighty love is near."*

When we let God direct our path, it's like being guided by the One who designed the map. The One who carved the valleys and raised the mountains. The One who knows every twist and turn because He drew them. Imagine being directed by the Creator Himself, the One who knows the end from the beginning. You can rest assured that you'll get to your destination safely and in one piece. That's why we're called to trust Him, not partially, not when it's easy, but with all our heart. Our understanding will fail us. God never will.

**Prayer**

**Heavenly Father, teach me to trust You with all my heart. In moments when I'm tempted to lean on my own understanding, remind me that Your wisdom is**

far greater than mine. Help me to acknowledge You in all my ways, big and small, and to recognise Your hand in every season of my life. Direct my paths, Lord. Lead me in the way I should go. And when doubt creeps in, anchor my faith in the truth that You know what is best for me. Thank You for being faithful even when I hesitate. I choose today to trust You fully, because You alone never fail. In Jesus' name, Amen.

# VERSE 4
# HEBREWS 12:1-2

*Therefore, since we are surrounded by such a huge crowd of witnesses to the life of faith, let us strip off every weight that slows us down, especially the sin that so easily trips us up. And let us run with endurance the race God has set before us. We do this by keeping our eyes on Jesus, the champion who initiates and perfects our faith. Because of the joy awaiting him, he endured the cross, disregarding its shame. Now he is seated in the place of honor beside God's throne.*

These verses come right after what has been described as the *"Hall of Faith"* – that remarkable chapter in Hebrews 11 that recounts the stories of those who walked by faith and pleased God. Hebrews 12 opens with a reminder that these men and women – Abraham, Moses, Joseph, Rahab, and so many others – are not just names in Scripture; they are witnesses to the life of faith. They surround us like spectators in a grand stadium, cheering us on as we run the race set before us. That image always encourages me. It tells me that I'm not alone. There's a cloud of witnesses, a heavenly audience, who understand what it means to endure, to believe even when it's hard, and to keep pressing forward.

But running this race of faith isn't easy. Along the way, we encounter hurdles and weights that slow us down. The writer tells us to *"strip off every weight that slows us down."* Imagine running a 100-meter dash with two 5kg dumbbells in your hands. No matter how fast you want to go, those weights will hold you back. In life, those weights can be many things – fear, doubt, unforgiveness, anxiety, guilt, even the opinions of others. And then there is sin, which doesn't just slow us down but actually trips us up. Sin distracts us, diverts us, and often causes us to fall flat on our faces.

But when we fall, that's not the end of the story. We can either stay down and lose the race, or we can get up, dust ourselves off, and keep running. The verse says, *"Let us run with endurance."* That word – endurance – speaks to consistency, determination, and resilience. It's not a sprint; it's a marathon. There are seasons where we'll feel strong, and others where every step feels heavy. But the call is the same: don't give up. Keep moving forward. God Himself has set this race before us, and He equips us with the strength to finish it.

The secret to running well, we're told, is to keep our eyes on Jesus. He is the champion of our faith – the one who not only began it but also perfects it. When I think of Jesus running His race, I am always humbled. He endured betrayal, mockery, and even the cross. Yet, He finished His course because He saw beyond the pain. *"Because of the joy awaiting Him,"* the Scripture says, *"He endured the cross."* That joy was the redemption of you and me – the joy of reconciling us to the Father. He disregarded the shame because He knew that at the finish line was victory, glory, and the place of honour at God's right hand.

It reminds me of watching athletes at the Olympics. You can see the intensity in their eyes; they're completely focused on the finish line. They don't look to their left or right; they run their own race. When they finally cross the line and mount the podium, that look of joy and fulfilment says it all. Their anthem is played, their country is proud, and their names are etched in history. That's the image of Jesus seated beside God's throne – victorious and glorified.

In our race, we're not competing against anyone else. The only competition is against ourselves – against the temptation to give up, to compare, to get distracted. Comparison is one of the greatest weights in life. When we start looking at other people's progress, we lose focus. That's why the Bible reminds us to *"stay in our lane."* Your journey is unique. The race God has set before you is different from mine. What matters is not how fast you run, but that you keep running faithfully.

Even in driving, we're taught that our car tends to follow the direction of our eyes. If we look left, we turn left; if we look right, we drift right. The same principle applies to life. Where our eyes go, our life follows. That's why we must keep our eyes on Jesus – not on the distractions, not on the noise, not on the people ahead or behind us, but on Him. Because when we focus on Him, everything else aligns. He becomes our strength when we're weary, our example when we're discouraged, and our joy when the road feels long.

So whatever stage of life you're in, remember: the race is not over. You may be tired, you may have stumbled, but get up and keep running. The witnesses are cheering, Jesus is waiting, and joy awaits at the finish line.

**Prayer**

Heavenly Father, thank You for setting before me the race of faith. Thank You for surrounding me with witnesses who remind me that it's possible to finish well. Lord, help me to lay aside every weight that slows me down - every fear, every distraction, and every sin that trips me up. Give me endurance to run with focus, courage, and grace. When I fall, help me to rise again. When I am weary, strengthen me. And most of all, help me to keep my eyes on Jesus — my example, my champion, and the perfecter of my faith. May I run faithfully until I reach the finish line, where the joy You have prepared for me awaits. In Jesus' name, Amen.

# VERSE 5
# JEREMIAH 29:11

*For I know the plans I have for you," says the Lord. "They are plans for good and not for disaster, to give you a future and a hope.*

This verse has always been one of my anchors in seasons of uncertainty and the unknown. It reminds me that God is not improvising with my life. He has a plan, and that plan is good. Sometimes, we get caught up in our own timelines, drafting five-year plans, mapping out our goals, and setting milestones for ourselves. And that's fine; planning is wise. The Bible even encourages us to plan. But this verse calls us to something deeper: trusting that God's plan overrides ours, and that His blueprint for our lives is infinitely better than what we could ever imagine.

God says, *"I know the plans I have for you."* Notice He doesn't say, *"I'm figuring them out as we go."* He knows. That means nothing happening to you or me takes Him by surprise. Even the detours, the delays, the disappointments, all of them are somehow woven into His master plan for our good.

The verse continues, *"They are plans for good and not for disaster."* This doesn't mean life will always be easy or pain-free. But it does mean that even the painful chapters are part of a larger story that leads to redemption. God's plans ultimately bring peace, joy, and purpose. His goodness isn't always seen in the moment; it's often understood in hindsight, when we look back and realise how He was protecting or preparing us all along.

Then He says, *"to give you a future and a hope."* That phrase always moves me. Hope is one of the most essential ingredients of life. When a person loses hope, they lose the strength to keep going. Hope tells you that even though today may not make sense, tomorrow holds promise. Hope gives you courage to wake up, to try again, to trust again. It reminds you that God is still writing your story.

As I go through this transition phase, stepping out of one major season and into another, not fully knowing what lies ahead, I take comfort in this verse. I may not have the full picture of what the next stage of my life looks like after the presidency or even after turning forty, but I know the One who holds the plan. So, I choose to rest in His knowledge, not my uncertainty. I choose His plan over mine, because His plans are for good and not for disaster. His plans give me a future and a hope. And that's all I need to keep moving forward with peace.

**Prayer**

**Lord, thank You for reminding me that You know the plans You have for me. When I am uncertain, help me to trust Your certainty. When I am restless, remind me that You are working for my good. Teach me to submit my plans to Yours and to find joy in the unfolding of Your will. As I walk into the next chapter of my life, let me not lean on my understanding but on Your promises. Give me the grace to trust that Your plans will lead me to a future filled with hope, peace, and purpose. In Jesus' name, Amen.**

# VERSE 6
# PSALM 23:1

*The Lord is my shepherd; I shall not want.*

I first learnt this verse back in primary school – Morning Star School. It was one of those Psalms we had to memorise alongside **Psalm 91** and **Psalm 121**. We could recite them so easily that they became part of our daily rhythm; spoken at school assemblies, during morning devotions, and in church. I remember singing **Psalm 23** in the Methodist Church and later at Prempeh College during Sunday services. But for many years, it was just words, a beautiful Psalm I knew by heart but not yet by experience.

That changed much later in life. When I was appointed as Legal Counsel to the President in 2017, this verse suddenly came alive. Many friends and even family friends cautioned me against accepting the appointment. Their concerns were not unfounded; they worried about the political atmosphere and the weight of responsibility, especially considering how young I was at the time.

But in prayer, the Lord reminded me of this verse. "T*he Lord is my shepherd; I shall not want.*" It was as though He whispered, "*You are not walking into this alone. I am your Shepherd.*"

A shepherd's duty is simple yet profound – to feed, to lead, to protect, and to provide. David understood this deeply. As a shepherd himself, he risked his life to protect his flock from lions and bears. So, when he called God his Shepherd, he wasn't speaking in poetic abstraction; he was describing a relationship of total trust. A shepherd makes sure his sheep never go hungry, never stray too far, and never face danger unguarded.

That's what God has been to me. There have been moments I didn't know how things would work out, moments when resources seemed thin, or when challenges loomed larger than my capacity, but He always made a way. I have seen doors open that I didn't even knock on. I have been led into green pastures when I least expected them. Truly, I lack nothing because the Lord has been my Shepherd.

So, when people ask how I'm managing, how I'm standing, how I keep going, I smile quietly because I know the answer; it's this verse. The Lord is my

Shepherd; I shall not want.

**Prayer**

**Lord, thank You for being my Shepherd, for leading me when I cannot see the path, for providing when I have no strength left to seek, and for protecting me when I don't even know I'm in danger. Teach me to trust You more deeply, to follow Your voice more closely, and to rest in the assurance that when You are my Shepherd, I shall not want. Help me walk daily in the peace that comes from knowing You are enough. In Jesus' name, Amen.**

# VERSE 7
# 2 CORINTHIANS 5:7

*For we walk by faith, not by sight.*

Faith was an abstract concept when I was growing up in the Church. I believed in God, I prayed, I read the Bible, and I was even born again, but faith? That was harder to grasp. I would hear people say "*walk by faith*" and wonder what that really meant in practical terms. How do you walk by something you cannot see? How do you trust something you cannot measure?

**Hebrews 11:1** gives a definition that is both profound and puzzling: "*Now faith is the substance of things hoped for, the evidence of things not seen.*" I must confess, even today, I am still unravelling the depth of that verse. But life has a way of teaching what theology alone cannot. Through my own journey, I have come to understand that walking by faith is choosing to trust God even when the path ahead makes no sense; it is choosing to believe His promises when your circumstances seem to contradict them.

I often say that 2017 was my year of faith. It was the year I saw firsthand what it truly meant to walk by faith and not by sight. I had switched jobs; from private practice into public service. It was a bold move, one that came with uncertainty. For months after the appointment, we were not paid any salaries, only a small weekly allowance to tide us over. I had used up all my savings, and my finances were running on empty. It was at that point that God began to teach me how to rely on Him fully.

When the first weekly allowance came after a couple of months, I was relieved. *"Finally,"* I thought, *"something to spend!"* But God had other plans. I remember vividly how He laid on my heart the principle of first fruits. The lawyer in me immediately began to argue with God, reasoning, analysing, calculating. But the Holy Spirit gently reminded me of His Word, and by the end of that evening, I was persuaded. That Friday night, I called my priest and went to see him. I knew if I waited till Sunday, I would spend the money. So, I handed over what would be my first income in my new role to God. It was all I had. The priest was astonished. He remarked that he had not seen such faith and prayed for me. I knew in my heart that I had done the right thing.

That act of obedience opened doors I could not have imagined. Growing up, I had seen my father live this kind of faith, giving when it made no logical sense. Once, when his brand-new car was involved in an accident, he gave the money he had saved for repairs to the church. I thought he was being irrational. But years later, I realised he was walking by faith, and soon after, God blessed him beyond measure.

In that same 2017, God continued to show Himself faithful. I moved out of my parents' house into my own place. Through a divine connection, I met Joseph Biga of Signum, another man of faith, who offered me shelter while he built a townhouse for me. There were moments I defaulted on payments, but Mr. Biga would always smile and say, "*My brother, don't worry about the money. God will provide.*" And indeed, He did.

That year, I also had my eye surgery in the U.S., and again, God provided. Later in the same year, I got married. When my wife and I counted the gifts and donations from our wedding day, the amount matched exactly what we owed our vendors. Not a cedi short, not a cedi more. We finished our wedding debt-free. By the end of 2017, I bought my first car. I look back and marvel at how many times I was tempted to worry, and yet God was already working behind the scenes.

To walk by faith and not by sight means learning to live beyond your senses. Sight will tell you there is no money in the account. Sight will tell you the odds are against you. Sight will remind you of your failures. But faith says, "*God is able.*" Faith says, "*It may not look like it now, but my Redeemer lives.*" Faith looks beyond the visible to the invisible hand of God at work.

Even the greatest men of God struggled with faith. John Wesley, for a long time, doubted whether he truly believed. Then his friend Peter Böhler gave him this timeless counsel: "*Preach faith till you have it; and then, because you have it, you will preach faith.*" In the same way, I say, *walk by faith till you have it; and then, because you have it, you will walk by faith.*

Faith is not a feeling. It is not optimism. It is obedience when it's hard. It is trust when the outcome is uncertain. It is surrender when you would rather take control. To walk by faith is to hand the pen of your story to God and trust Him to write it better than you ever could.

## Prayer

Heavenly Father, thank You for teaching me what it means to walk by faith and not by sight. Thank You for every season that tested my trust and every moment You proved Yourself faithful. Strengthen my faith, Lord, especially when I am tempted to doubt. Help me to see with spiritual eyes and not be ruled by what I see around me. Let my life continually reflect Your faithfulness, and may my steps be guided by Your Word and Your Spirit. Teach me to walk in faith until it becomes second nature, until every decision, every move, and every breath reflects total trust in You. In Jesus' name, Amen.

# VERSE 8
# 2 CORINTHIANS 4:18

*So we fix our eyes not on what is seen, but on what is unseen, since what is seen is temporary, but what is unseen is eternal.*

This verse is one of the most profound truths about the Christian Walk. It reminds us that the visible world, with all its pleasures, struggles, accolades, and pain, is fleeting. What truly matters lies beyond what our natural eyes can perceive. In our daily lives, we are surrounded by things that demand our attention – success, reputation, wealth, influence, and even the challenges that seem to overwhelm us. Yet, Scripture calls us to look deeper – to fix our eyes not on what is seen, but on what is unseen.

When I served as Legal Counsel to the President, this verse became an anchor for my soul. It served as my compass. In that environment, it was easy to get caught up in the power, the prestige, the politics, and the constant activity around national leadership. But early on, I realised how temporary all those things were. The meetings, the ceremonies, the influence – they all had an expiry date. What truly mattered was not how much authority one carried in the moment, but whether one was walking in obedience to God's will.

That realization shaped how I approached every decision, every challenge, and every opportunity. I printed this verse and placed it on the wall in my office as a daily reminder that the unseen – integrity, faith, humility, righteousness, obedience, and eternal purpose – mattered far more than the seen. Because what is seen is temporary, but what is unseen is eternal.

Fixing our eyes on the unseen doesn't mean ignoring the realities around us; it means interpreting them through the lens of eternity. It means understanding that trials are not just inconveniences; they are training grounds for our faith. Success is not an end in itself; it's a platform to glorify God. Relationships are not merely social connections; they are opportunities to reflect God's love.

In truth, the Christian life is about vision; not with our physical eyes, but with the eyes of faith. When we fix our eyes on what is unseen, we begin to live differently. We stop chasing applause and start pursuing purpose. We stop worrying about what people think and start caring about what God thinks. We stop clinging to what fades and start investing in what lasts forever.

So, I encourage you: *fix your eyes on the things that are unseen* – the things of God, the things that nurture your spirit, the things that keep you in His will. That is where true peace and eternal reward are found.

**Prayer**

**Heavenly Father, thank You for reminding me that what is seen is temporary, but what is unseen is eternal. Help me to fix my eyes on You and not be distracted by the fleeting things of this world. Teach me to value what matters most - righteousness, faith, love, and obedience. Strengthen me to walk by faith and not by sight, to live each day with eternity in mind. May my actions, thoughts, and desires align with Your eternal purpose for my life. In Jesus' name, Amen.**

# VERSE 9
# ISAIAH 41:10

*Fear not, for I am with you; Be not dismayed, for I am your God. I will strengthen you, Yes, I will help you, I will uphold you with My righteous right hand.*

This verse is one of the most comforting promises in Scripture. It reminds us of God's abiding presence and His unshakable commitment to those who trust in Him. It begins with a divine command, *"Fear not."* God isn't merely suggesting that we try to avoid fear; He's commanding us not to fear because fear contradicts faith. But God never gives an instruction without also providing the reason or assurance to make it possible. Here, the assurance is powerful: *"for I am with you."*

That short phrase changes everything. When we know that God is with us, our perspective shifts. The storms of life don't suddenly disappear, but we are no longer alone in facing them. Whether it's the fear of failure, loss, rejection, or uncertainty about the future, God's presence assures us that we can endure, overcome, and even grow through it all.

He goes further to say, *"Be not dismayed, for I am your God."* This means we don't have to be discouraged or lose heart when things look impossible. God isn't some distant deity observing from afar; He is our God, intimately involved in every detail of our lives. That relationship changes everything. Because He is our God, we can face tomorrow with hope, even when today feels unbearable.

The verse then builds on that assurance with three promises that cover every human need:
- *"I will strengthen you"* – when we are weak, drained, and weary.
- *"Yes, I will help you"* – when the burden feels too heavy or we do not know what to do.
- *"I will uphold you with My righteous right hand"* – when we are falling or when life seems to crumble beneath us.

Each promise is layered, showing God not only as our protector but also as our sustainer. He doesn't just watch us from a distance; He gets involved. He strengthens, helps, and upholds. The *"righteous right hand"* symbolises His power, authority, and justice –

it's the same hand that formed the heavens, delivered Israel, and raised Jesus from the dead. That's the hand holding you up even when you feel like you're about to break. When you think about it like that, doesn't it feel good?

I remember encouraging my father with this verse during a difficult season in our family. He was quiet for a moment and then said in Fante, "*Ɔyɛ ampa, na Isaiah nsɛm wɔ hɔ pa pa pa*" - "*It's true; there are many nuggets in Isaiah.*" He was right. This single verse alone carries enough hope to steady anyone's heart. It teaches us that no matter how uncertain life becomes, whether through our own mistakes, external challenges, or unexplainable loss, God's grip on us does not loosen.

So, when fear rises, when confusion clouds your mind, when you feel overwhelmed by expectations or setbacks, remember **Isaiah 41:10.** Say it aloud. Let it sink deep into your spirit. Fear loses its power in the presence of faith, and faith is strengthened by the reminder that God is with you.

**Prayer**

Heavenly Father, thank You for the assurance of Your presence. When fear tries to take hold of our hearts, remind us that You are near. When we grow weary, strengthen us. When we stumble, uphold us with Your righteous right hand. Help us to rest in the truth that You are our God, faithful, powerful, and ever-present. Teach us to trust You completely, to release our fears, and to walk boldly in faith. In Jesus' name, Amen.

# VERSE 10
# ISAIAH 40:31

*But those who wait on the Lord shall renew their strength; They shall mount up with wings like eagles, They shall run and not be weary, They shall walk and not faint.*

Waiting on the Lord is among the most difficult yet rewarding disciplines in the life of a believer. It is not passive waiting – it is an active posture of faith, trust, and expectation. It is the kind of waiting that keeps you anchored when nothing seems to be moving, when your prayers seem unanswered, and when life feels like it's passing you by.

Waiting on the Lord can be exhausting. You can wait and get tired. You can wait and feel forgotten. You can wait and begin to wonder if God has heard you at all. Yet, this verse assures us that those who wait on the Lord shall renew their strength. It's a paradox; while you wait, you are renewed. The world sees waiting as inactivity, but in God's economy, waiting is preparation. He strengthens you in the waiting. He matures you in the waiting. He builds your faith, your patience, and your character in the waiting.

In our everyday lives, waiting takes many forms. You may be waiting for a job opportunity, for a promotion, for healing, for marriage, for a child, or even for clarity about your purpose. The waiting season can feel lonely and painful, especially when others seem to be racing ahead. You see your peers getting married, buying homes, building businesses, winning awards, and you can't help but wonder if God has forgotten about you. But this verse reminds us that God's timing is perfect and His process is purposeful.

I remember when I was selected as a Global Shaper of the World Economic Forum in the Accra Hub. I looked around and felt completely inadequate. Everyone seemed so accomplished; they were entrepreneurs, innovators, and leaders making waves in their fields. I was just an Associate in a law firm in Accra. I told the curator, my good friend Fred Deegbe Jnr., that I felt out of place. Fred looked at me and said, "That's exactly why you're here. You bring something none of us have, and you're right where you need to be."

At the time, I didn't understand what he meant. I thought he was just being kind. But years later, when

I was appointed Legal Counsel to the President of Ghana, a position that opened doors to the same World Economic Forum I once felt unworthy of, Fred came to my office to take my shoe measurements for my traditional wedding and reminded me of that conversation. Only then did it make sense. I finally understood. God had been preparing me quietly. While I was waiting, He was aligning circumstances, shaping character, and preparing me for elevation.

This is what it means to mount up with wings like eagles. Eagles don't flap endlessly like other birds. They soar, they rise higher by catching the wind that others resist. Those who wait on God learn to soar above life's turbulence, not by striving, but by trusting. And when they run, they do not grow weary, because the strength they run with is not their own. It is renewed strength, divine strength.

So, if you are in a season of waiting, take heart. God has not forgotten you. He is renewing your strength. You may not see it, but He is preparing you for a moment when you will rise and realise why you had to wait. The same people who ran ahead may grow weary, but you, because you waited on the Lord, will keep walking and not faint.

**Prayer**

Heavenly Father, thank You for the promise that those who wait on You shall renew their strength. Teach me to wait with patience and faith, even when I cannot see what You are doing. Strengthen my heart when I grow weary, and help me trust that Your timing is perfect. Lord, let me soar like an eagle above every storm. Renew my vision, my purpose, and my hope. And when You lift me up, remind me always that it was Your grace that sustained me through the waiting. In Jesus' name, Amen.

# VERSE 11
# HEBREWS 13:5

*Don't love money; be satisfied with what you have.*
*For God has said, "I will never fail you. I will never*
*abandon you."*

This verse speaks deeply to the human condition. In a world where success is often measured by wealth, possessions, and status, this verse draws our hearts back to what truly matters: trust in God's presence and sufficiency. Money in itself is not evil; it is a tool. But the love of money, the desire to accumulate, to compare, to compete, can quietly enslave the soul. When our hearts become entangled in that pursuit, peace departs, and contentment becomes a stranger.

When I served as Legal Counsel to the President, this verse served as a daily reminder of who truly provides. I had it pasted on my wall to remind myself that even in an environment where influence, access, and power can easily breed greed, the Lord calls us to contentment. There is a public perception that anyone who serves in high office must be chasing wealth or personal gain. It is a dangerous assumption that can tempt even the most well-meaning person to prove it true. But this verse anchored me. It reminded me that I did not need to pursue wealth to prove my worth or to secure my future. My Shepherd had already promised that I would not want.

It taught me to be content, not complacent, but content. To appreciate what God had placed in my hands at that moment, trusting that He knew what was best for me. It taught me not to compare my journey with that of others, not to envy their possessions, their titles, or their lifestyles, but to remain grounded in gratitude. The world will always present us with reasons to feel inadequate: someone will always have more, earn more, travel more, or appear to be more successful. But God's Word reminds us that contentment is not in having much; it is in knowing that God is with you.

The verse ends with one of the most comforting promises in all of Scripture: "*I will never fail you. I will never abandon you.*" This is not a vague assurance; it is a divine guarantee from the Creator Himself. God is saying, "*I am enough.*" Even when the bank account is low, even when the opportunities seem scarce, even when others seem to be racing ahead, God's presence is the constant that sustains us. He has never failed His children in Scripture, and He will not start with you.

In every season of life, whether in abundance or in need, this verse is an anchor. It reminds us that our joy, our peace, and our confidence do not come from money, position, or possessions, but from the faithful presence of God who promises never to leave us nor forsake us.

**Prayer**

**Heavenly Father, thank You for the reminder that You are my ultimate provider. Teach me to find contentment in You alone and not in the things of this world. Guard my heart from the love of money, from greed, and from comparison. Help me to trust in Your provision and to rest in the assurance that You will never fail me nor abandon me. When I am tempted to chase after worldly gain, draw me back to Your Word and remind me that in You, I have all that I need. In Jesus' name, Amen.**

# VERSE 12
# ECCLESIASTES 9:11

*I have observed something else under the sun. The fastest runner doesn't always win the race, and the strongest warrior doesn't always win the battle. The wise sometimes go hungry, and the skillful are not necessarily wealthy. And those who are educated don't always lead successful lives. It is all decided by chance, by being in the right place at the right time.*

This profound observation comes from Solomon, the wisest man who ever lived. It is one of the most humbling and thought-provoking verses in Scripture because it reminds us that life does not always follow human logic or predictable outcomes. Solomon had seen enough of life to realise that ability, strength, and even wisdom are not always the ultimate determinants of success.

He begins by saying that the fastest runner doesn't always win the race. This challenges the common assumption that speed automatically guarantees victory. Sometimes, the runner may stumble.

Sometimes, the weather may change. Sometimes, the race may not even favour speed but endurance. In other words, talent and preparation matter, but there are unseen variables – time and chance – that can alter outcomes.

He continues, the strongest warrior doesn't always win the battle. Strength is good, but it is not absolute. Strategy, timing, and favour play their roles. There are countless stories of underdogs who overcame giants because the circumstances turned in their favour, or, as Solomon puts it, because they were in the right place at the right time. Solomon's own father, David, is a typical example of someone who won the battle being the underdog.

He goes further to say that the wise sometimes go hungry, and the skillful are not necessarily wealthy. This is perhaps the most relatable part. Many of us have met people with extraordinary wisdom, intelligence, or skills who are still struggling to make ends meet. It is not always because they lack effort or discipline; sometimes, it is because they have not yet encountered that divine moment of alignment, when preparation meets opportunity.

Finally, he says, those who are educated don't always lead successful lives. Education is valuable and should be pursued diligently, but it is not the sole predictor of success. There are countless educated people who remain unfulfilled, and there are others with little formal education who build empires and leave legacies.

So, what is Solomon teaching us here? That beyond our human abilities, success often depends on divine orchestration, being in the right place at the right time. It is a reminder that we must seek more than just skill, wisdom, and education; we must seek discernment to know where to be and when to move.

Early in my professional life, I recognised how true this verse was. I noticed that being in the right place at the right time often determined career progression and opportunity, just as being in the wrong place at the wrong time could lead to trouble, disgrace, or even death. Little did I know that this principle was already recorded in Scripture as an observation of Solomon himself.

Looking back, I can see how this truth has played out in my own journey. I was not the most brilliant lawyer. I never worked with the President when he was in private practice, and I had no prior professional encounter with him. There were many others who could have been chosen to serve as his Legal Counsel, including those who had worked with him directly. Yet, somehow, I was the one appointed. I believe that was a divine alignment, God positioning me at the right place at the right time.

This verse, therefore, teaches us humility and dependence on God. It reminds us that we are not the masters of our own outcomes. We may prepare, study, train, and strategise, and we should, but in the end, it is God who determines times and seasons. As Christians, our prayer should not only be for wisdom and skill but also for divine timing and positioning. When these align, our gifts flourish and our efforts bear fruit.

**Prayer**

**Heavenly Father, thank You for the wisdom in Your Word that reminds us that success is not solely about speed, strength, or intellect, but about Your divine timing and favour. Teach us to trust in Your seasons and to discern the right place and the right time in every area of our lives. Align our steps with Your purpose, and let every skill, talent, and opportunity You have given us find its proper place under Your direction. May we never rely solely on our strength but always on Your guidance and grace. In Jesus' name, Amen.**

# VERSE 13
# JOB 42:10

*When Job prayed for his friends, the Lord restored his fortunes. In fact, the Lord gave him twice as much as before!*

This verse conveys a reflective truth about restoration, humility, and intercession. Job had lost everything – his wealth, his children, his health, his reputation. Even his friends, who should have been a source of comfort, misunderstood him and accused him of wrongdoing. Yet, when the time came for God to restore Job, the trigger was not Job's personal cry for help, not his attempt to rebuild his wealth, nor his demand for justice. The turning point came when Job prayed for his friends.

That act alone reveals the true state of Job's heart. Despite being wronged and criticised, he chose forgiveness over bitterness, and intercession over resentment. It was at that precise moment, when Job looked beyond his pain and prayed for others, that God stepped in to restore him. Not only was Job restored, but he was given double of what he had before.

In today's world, the message of this verse runs counter to everything society promotes. We are taught to chase success, build our empires, and climb higher, often at the expense of others. Some even find satisfaction in seeing their peers struggle so they can remain the "*successful one*" in the group. That mindset is rooted in pride and insecurity. God, however, delights in hearts that are generous, compassionate, and selfless. When we genuinely desire the success of others and pray for our friends, even those who may have wronged us, we align ourselves with God's nature.

I have always found this verse deeply personal. I have seen firsthand that life is not about outshining others but about walking together in mutual upliftment. I often say jokingly, but with sincerity, that I would love to see all my friends wealthy, flourishing, and blessed. That way, we can all enjoy life without discomfort or pretence. It brings me great joy when those around me prosper. And I have come to understand that one of the most powerful ways to open the door to our own restoration is to pray for the well-being of our friends.

When Job prayed for his friends, something shifted in the spiritual realm. His situation turned around. So let us cultivate that same posture, to intercede for our friends, to wish them well, to cover them in prayer, and to rejoice when they prosper. Because in God's economy, generosity of heart always precedes multiplication of blessings.

**Prayer**

**Heavenly Father, thank You for the lesson in Job's story. Today, I lift up my friends before You, every one of them, near and far. I pray that You bless them with peace, wisdom, health, and abundance. Restore what they may have lost, strengthen their faith, and grant them double for every trouble they've endured. May their homes overflow with laughter, their hands never lack, and their hearts always be full of joy. And as You bless them, Lord, remember me also. Restore what needs to be restored in my life, and let Your favour surround us all. In Jesus' name, Amen.**

# VERSE 14
# MATTHEW 6:34

*So don't worry about tomorrow, for tomorrow will bring its own worries. Today's trouble is enough for today.*

A powerful continuation of Jesus' teaching in the Sermon on the Mount. It comes right after His reminder to seek first the Kingdom of God and His righteousness, with the assurance that all other things, our needs, our provisions, our future, will be added unto us. Then He adds this final piece of wisdom: *don't worry about tomorrow*. It sounds simple, yet it is one of the hardest things to do as humans.

As people, we are natural planners. We think ahead. We prepare. But sometimes, our thinking ahead crosses the fine line between planning and worrying. We begin to fret about what the next week holds, what our next career step will be, how our children will turn out, what the economy will look like, whether we will have enough to retire on, or even what will happen five years down the line. We lose sleep over things that haven't even happened yet.

This verse reminds us to stay anchored in the present. It's as if Jesus is saying, *"You have enough on your plate today. Handle that. Tomorrow will come with its own set of issues, and when it does, I'll still be there."* Worrying about tomorrow doesn't solve tomorrow's problems; it only drains today's strength.

When I reflect on this verse, I recall the advice my father gave me when I was young, which was later echoed by the President when I worked with him: *"If you can do something today, do it; don't wait until tomorrow."* That simple advice carries profound wisdom. It aligns perfectly with this teaching from Jesus. Deal with today's responsibilities. Solve today's problems. Take today's opportunities. Let tomorrow take care of itself when it arrives, because God will still be God tomorrow.

There is also a deeper spiritual message here. This verse calls us to trust God completely. It reminds us that worrying is a quiet way of saying we don't fully believe God will handle our future. When we trust Him, we acknowledge that He is already in tomorrow, preparing the way for us. We may not know what tomorrow holds, but we can rest in the truth that He holds tomorrow.

Every day comes with its own challenges, but it also comes with its own grace. The same God who gives us strength for today will provide strength for tomorrow. Therefore, live one day at a time, fully present, fully trusting, and fully at peace.

**Prayer**

**Heavenly Father, thank You for reminding me that You are in control of both today and tomorrow. Teach me to trust You more deeply and to live one day at a time. Help me not to be consumed by anxiety about the future, but to rest in the assurance that You are already there. Give me the wisdom to handle today's challenges with Your strength and the faith to believe that tomorrow will take care of itself under Your watchful eye. In Jesus' name, Amen.**

# VERSE 15
# ACTS 13:36

*This is not a reference to David,* **for after David had done the will of God in his own generation, he died** *and was buried with his ancestors, and his body decayed.*

This verse might appear ordinary at first glance, a simple reference to David's life and death. But when you pause and reflect on the words, especially the part that says "*after David had done the will of God in his own generation*", you realise it carries one of the most profound truths about human existence and purpose.

I first heard this verse while driving to work one morning, listening to The Purpose Driven Life by Pastor Rick Warren. As he mentioned it, those words, "*after David had done the will of God in his own generation*", seemed to leap out of the speakers and take root in my heart. I couldn't shake them off. They became a defining lens through which I began to view life, purpose, and calling.

It suddenly dawned on me that God has a purpose for every generation, and for each of us within that generation. Every era has its challenges, its opportunities, and its divine assignments. And in every generation, God raises people who are meant to carry out His will; people who stand in the gap, advance His kingdom, defend truth, and leave the world better than they met it. David was one of them. He lived at a particular time, faced his share of trials and triumphs, and fulfilled the will of God for that time. After that, his work was done.

This means that we, too, have been placed in our generation for a reason. None of us is here by accident. The place, the period, and the people we are surrounded by are all part of God's grand design. The real question is: What is God's will for me in this generation? And am I doing it?

For me, this verse became a reminder that I must not just exist or succeed by worldly standards; I must do the will of God in my generation. That means identifying what burdens God has placed on my heart for this time and using the gifts, platforms, and opportunities He's given me to fulfil His purpose. Whether in governance, law, leadership, writing, or ministry, whatever sphere of influence God has entrusted us, we must ask daily: *Lord, am I doing Your will in my generation?*

David didn't live a perfect life, but he lived a purposeful one. His heart was aligned with God's. He sought forgiveness when he failed and direction when he was lost. And when his race was done, Scripture records that he *"had done the will of God in his own generation."* What a testimony to aspire to! That when our lives are over, it will be said of us too, not that we accumulated wealth or gained fame, but that we did the will of God in our time.

This verse has since anchored my perspective on purpose. It reminds me that life is short, and our time here is finite. The true measure of a life well-lived is whether we fulfilled God's purpose before our days are done. And thankfully, we are not left to figure that out on our own; the Holy Spirit is our guide. He nudges, convicts, and directs us toward what God wants us to accomplish.

So, I live with that constant awareness: *I am here for a divine assignment.* My generation has its share of darkness, confusion, and need. And just like David, I must rise to do God's will before my time on earth is over.

## Prayer

Heavenly Father, thank You for reminding us through Your Word that we are created to do Your will in our generation. Just as David fulfilled Your purpose in his time, help us to discover and walk in the purpose You designed for us. Open our eyes to see the work You have called us to do, give us the wisdom to discern Your will, and grant us the courage and strength to carry it out faithfully. May our lives bring glory to Your name, and when our journey on earth is done, may it be said of us that we did Your will in our generation. In Jesus' mighty name, we pray. Amen.

# VERSE 16
# PHILIPPIANS 4:6-7

*Be anxious for nothing, but in everything by prayer and supplication, with thanksgiving, let your requests be made known to God; and the peace of God, which surpasses all understanding, will guard your hearts and minds through Christ Jesus.*

A powerful and comforting verse in the Bible, and one that I personally hold very dear, especially in seasons when my heart is burdened, and there's so much uncertainty around me. It has been an anchor for my mind and emotions, especially during transitions, challenges, and times when things simply did not make sense.

Paul's message to the Philippians begins with a clear and liberating command: *"Be anxious for nothing."* Living in this world without moments of worry is almost impossible, but the Bible doesn't just tell us not to worry; it tells us what to do instead. Anxiety feeds on uncertainty and fear, but prayer feeds on faith and trust. When we shift our focus from what might go wrong to Who is in control, our entire perspective changes.

Paul continues: *"But in everything, by prayer and supplication, with thanksgiving, let your requests be made known to God."* This verse gives us a divine exchange system; God invites us to trade our anxiety for His peace. We do this through prayer, supplication, and thanksgiving. Prayer is the conversation, supplication is the heartfelt request, and thanksgiving is the faith-filled attitude that says, *"God, I trust You even before I see the outcome."*

When I have heavy decisions to make, or when the future looks uncertain, as it sometimes does even after leaving a significant role or season in life, I turn to this verse. There were times after leaving office when people asked, *"What are you going to do next?"* or *"How will you sustain yourself and your family?"* These were genuine questions, but I found peace in the truth of **Philippians 4:6–7.** The Word says be anxious for nothing, and I took that literally. I told myself, If God has brought me this far, He will not abandon me now.

It is through that mindset of prayer and thanksgiving that I have experienced what Paul describes next:

*"the peace of God, which surpasses all understanding."* This peace is not logical. It doesn't align with your bank balance, job status, medical report, or external circumstances. It's that calm you can't explain; the smile you wear when life says you should be crying; the steady faith you carry when everyone expects you to panic. That's the peace of God. It surpasses understanding because it is divine. It's not based on reasoning; it's rooted in relationship.

And Paul adds that this peace will *"guard your hearts and minds through Christ Jesus."* That's powerful imagery. God's peace is not passive; it's active. It stands guard like a soldier over your heart and mind, keeping anxiety, fear, and despair from breaking through. When the enemy tries to sow seeds of worry or doubt, the peace of God becomes your shield.

I've come to realise that anxiety often comes from trying to control what only God can handle. The moment you surrender your worries through prayer and thanksgiving, God steps in with His supernatural peace. It's like taking a deep breath in the middle of a storm and realising you're safe because He's in the boat with you.

So, if you are someone who worries a lot about the

future, finances, career, relationships, or even the direction of your life, anchor yourself in this verse. Don't suppress your worries; surrender them. Don't ignore your fears; hand them to God in prayer. And as you do, thank Him in advance for what He's already doing behind the scenes. You will begin to feel that quiet assurance, that inexplicable calm, that beautiful peace that only He can give.

**Prayer**

**Heavenly Father, thank You for Your Word that reminds us not to be anxious for anything. Today, we surrender every worry, fear, and uncertainty to You. Teach us to bring everything to You in prayer and with thanksgiving. Fill our hearts with faith and our minds with peace. Let Your peace, which surpasses all understanding, guard our hearts and minds through Christ Jesus. Help us to trust You even when we cannot see the way ahead, knowing that You are faithful and in control. May we live anchored in Your peace every single day. In Jesus' name, Amen.**

# VERSE 17
# PHILIPPIANS 4:8

*Finally, brethren, whatsoever things are true, whatsoever things are honest, whatsoever things are just, whatsoever things are pure, whatsoever things are lovely, whatsoever things are of good report; if there be any virtue, and if there be any praise, think on these things.*

This is a profound verse about the power of the mind and the kind of thoughts that should occupy the heart of a believer. The Apostle Paul, writing from prison, gives us not just a list but a mental framework, a divine filter for our thought life. He teaches that peace and victory begin with what we choose to think about.

For me, I had never truly paid attention to this verse until I met my wife, Lady-Ann. This happens to be one of her favourite verses, and through her, I began to understand it more deeply. It is a verse about mental discipline and spiritual focus. It teaches that as believers, we must be intentional about our thoughts.

Every time a thought enters our minds, we should measure it against the attributes Paul lists here.

Are my thoughts true – or are they rooted in fear, lies, or assumptions?
Are they honest – or am I justifying something I know isn't right?
Are they just – do they align with righteousness and fairness?
Are they pure – untainted by lust, pride, or greed?
Are they lovely – do they reflect the beauty of God's love and grace?
Are they of good report – would I be proud to share them before God?

Paul concludes by saying, *"if there be any virtue, and if there be any praise, think on these things."* This is not just advice, it's a command. It is a spiritual practice that shapes how we see the world and how we respond to it.

In our current world, this command could not be more critical. We live in an age where the mind is under constant attack. The media, social platforms, and even casual conversations often promote negativity, fear, lust, greed, envy, and comparison. If we are not careful, we can unknowingly begin to dwell on these things. The human mind was not designed to handle so much unfiltered information, and when we allow darkness to fill our thoughts, it affects our emotions, our health, and even our faith.

But Paul gives us a way out. He tells us to consciously choose our thoughts, to replace lies with truth, negativity with praise, and impurity with purity. This is not just positive thinking; it is spiritual warfare of the mind.

That's where **2 Corinthians 10:4–5** comes in to complete this truth:

> *"For the weapons of our warfare are not carnal, but mighty through God to the pulling down of strongholds; casting down imaginations, and every high thing that exalteth itself against the knowledge of God, and bringing into captivity every thought to the obedience of Christ."*

This verse reveals that our thoughts are not harmless; they are the battleground of spiritual warfare. A stronghold is a mindset or pattern of thinking that contradicts God's truth. It could be fear, insecurity, pride, or hopelessness that keeps us trapped. But through Christ, we have divine power to pull down these strongholds. We are not powerless victims of our thoughts; we are called to take every thought captive and make it obedient to Christ.

That means when a thought of fear comes, we confront it with God's Word: *"God has not given me the spirit of fear."*
When a thought of condemnation arises, we respond: *"There is therefore now no condemnation for those who are in Christ Jesus."*
When the enemy whispers doubt, we declare: *"I can do all things through Christ who strengthens me."*

This is how we *"think on these things"* in a world full of noise and negativity. We do not passively accept every thought; we filter, fight, and focus. We use the Word of God as our weapon to bring our minds under divine order.

In truth, it's not easy. The mind often wanders, and we all face moments of mental struggle. But this is why Paul also says in **Romans 12:2**, *"Be transformed by the renewing of your mind."* The renewal of the mind is a daily practice, allowing God's Word and the Holy Spirit to reshape how we think, perceive, and respond. Over time, our thoughts begin to align more naturally with the character of Christ.

When we train our minds to dwell on truth, honesty, purity, and love, we begin to see life differently. Peace becomes possible. Joy becomes consistent. Our hearts become lighter. And we begin to experience the kind of inner calm that only God can give.

So, let us guard our minds with the same care we guard our homes. Let us not allow every voice, video, or opinion to plant seeds in our thoughts. Instead, let us think on what is true and cast down every imagination that exalts itself against the knowledge of God. When we do this, we win not only the battle of the mind but also the battle of the heart.

**Prayer**

**Heavenly Father, thank You for reminding us of the power of our thoughts. Help us to guard our minds diligently and to fill them only with what is true, honest, just, pure, lovely, and of good report. When negative or sinful thoughts arise, give us the strength to cast them down and bring them into obedience to Christ. Teach us to use Your Word as our weapon to destroy strongholds in our minds. Renew our thinking daily through Your Spirit, and grant us the peace that surpasses understanding. May our thoughts, words, and actions reflect Your truth and glory. In Jesus' name, Amen.**

# VERSE 18
# PHILIPPIANS 4:13

*I can do all things through Christ who strengthens me.*

This is an empowering declaration that speaks directly to our human limitations and reminds us that divine strength is available to those who trust in Christ. The verse is not merely about achieving goals or accomplishing dreams; it's about dependence, recognising that our ability to endure, excel, and overcome comes not from our strength but from Christ, who empowers us.

When Paul wrote these words, he was not living in comfort or success. He was in prison. Yet, in that confined space, he had found an inner strength that surpassed circumstance, a strength rooted in Christ. This tells us that the verse is not only about achieving great things, but also about enduring difficult things. It is about thriving in weakness because Christ's power is made perfect in our weakness.

For me personally, this verse became a lifeline during one of the most defining moments of my professional life, when I was appointed as Legal Counsel to the President of Ghana. Being the first and youngest person to ever hold that position, I was both honoured and overwhelmed. There was no blueprint to follow, no handbook to consult, and no predecessor to call for advice. The weight of the responsibility was heavy. Every decision carried national implications. At times, I questioned whether I was ready, whether I truly belonged there.

That's when **Philippians 4:13** became more than just a verse. It became a reality. Whenever I doubted myself, I prayed, and this verse echoed in my spirit: *"You can do all things through Christ who strengthens you."* It reminded me that my adequacy was not in my experience, my training, or my background, but in Christ. I didn't need to have it all figured out; I just needed to stay connected to the One who gives strength.

This verse applies to every area of our lives, whether you're a student facing exams, a parent raising children, an entrepreneur building a business, or someone battling through a difficult season. It tells us that no task, no challenge, no calling is too big when

Christ is the source of our strength. It also humbles us to remember that we can do nothing of eternal significance without Him.

The keyword in the verse is "*through.*" It reminds us that our strength flows through Christ, not through ourselves. He is the channel. When we depend on Him, through prayer, faith, and obedience, His strength sustains us. That is why Paul didn't say, *"I can do all things because I'm strong."* He said, *"I can do all things through Christ who strengthens me."*

So, the next time you face a challenge that feels beyond your ability, remember that it's not beyond God's ability in you. The same Christ, who strengthened Paul in prison, who strengthened me in the corridors of high office, and who strengthens millions around the world daily, will strengthen you too.

**Prayer**

**Heavenly Father, thank You for reminding me that I can do all things through Christ who strengthens me. When I feel inadequate, remind me that Your strength is made perfect in my weakness. Help me to**

depend on You fully and to draw my confidence from Your presence, not my own ability. Strengthen me today in my work, in my relationships, and in every challenge I face. Let Your power flow through me so that everything I do brings glory to Your name. In Jesus' name, I pray. Amen.

# VERSE 19
# JAMES 1:5

*If you need wisdom, ask our generous God, and he will give it to you. He will not rebuke you for asking.*

A reassuring promise in Scripture that reminds us that wisdom is not a human construct; it is a divine gift. The verse begins with a condition: *"If you need wisdom."* That statement alone acknowledges that there are times when we will lack clarity, when our own understanding will not be enough, and when our experience or education cannot provide the right answers. But God, in His love, provides a solution: ask Him.

When I discovered this verse, it became one of my favourite prayers. I still remember when I first started using it intentionally in my prayer life. I would say, *"Lord, Your Word says if I lack wisdom, I should ask You. I am asking now. Please give me wisdom for this situation."* That simple prayer has been transformative. Whenever I've faced complex decisions, especially in my career, I have seen God's hand guiding my thoughts and words.

When I became Legal Counsel to the President, the demands were beyond anything I had previously experienced. I was young, and many of those I advised were older and far more experienced in public administration. There was no manual or predecessor to follow. I knew that to succeed, I would need wisdom beyond human reasoning. So, I turned to this verse daily. I prayed for wisdom before major meetings, before preparing sensitive memos, and before advising the President on constitutional issues. Over time, people began to comment: *"You speak with such wisdom,"* or *"Your judgment is sound."* I knew it was not because I was the most intelligent or experienced but because God had answered my prayer for wisdom.

James tells us that God is generous. He doesn't give wisdom in small doses or measure it sparingly. He gives it freely and abundantly to those who ask sincerely. And He *"will not rebuke you for asking."* That means no matter how often we come back to Him for guidance, He doesn't tire of our questions or our dependence. Unlike people who may grow impatient when we seek help repeatedly, God delights when His children come to Him for direction.

This verse beautifully connects with the story of King Solomon in **1 Kings 3** and **2 Chronicles 1**. When God appeared to Solomon and told him to ask for anything, Solomon did not request wealth, power, or fame. Instead, he said, *"Give me wisdom and knowledge, that I may lead this people, for who is able to govern this great people of Yours?"* God was so pleased with that request that He not only gave Solomon unmatched wisdom but also blessed him with riches and honour beyond measure. Solomon's example teaches us that when we prioritise wisdom, especially wisdom to serve others and fulfil our purpose, God responds with blessings that go beyond our expectations.

In our modern lives, wisdom is more valuable than ever. We live in an age of information, but not necessarily wisdom. Many people have knowledge, data, and opinions, yet lack discernment, the ability to make right judgments. Wisdom helps us know when to speak, how to act, and what to do in difficult moments. It's wisdom that helps us navigate complex relationships, lead with integrity, and remain calm in times of crisis.

So, I encourage you to ask God for wisdom at whatever stage of life you are in, whether you are facing a major decision, leading a team, managing a family, or trying to understand your next step. He is ready to give it to you freely. And remember: when God gives wisdom, He also gives peace to go with it.

**Prayer**

**Heavenly Father, Thank You for being a generous God who gives wisdom freely to all who ask. Today, I humbly come before You, asking for divine wisdom in every area of my life. Teach me to make the right decisions, to discern truth from error, and to walk in integrity and understanding. Just as You granted wisdom to Solomon, grant me insight and clarity to fulfil the purpose You have placed before me. Let Your wisdom guide my thoughts, my words, and my actions. In Jesus' mighty name, I pray.**

# VERSE 20
# JAMES 1:2-4

*Dear brothers and sisters, when troubles of any kind come your way, consider it an opportunity for great joy. For you know that when your faith is tested, your endurance has a chance to grow. So let it grow, for when your endurance is fully developed, you will be perfect and complete, needing nothing.*

One of the most counterintuitive passages in all of Scripture. It truly contradicts human logic. Who, in their right mind, looks at trouble and says, *"Here comes an opportunity for great joy!"* Not even joy, but great joy. It doesn't make sense from a human standpoint. But that's exactly what James is calling us to do.

He is not saying if troubles come; he says when they come. It is a certainty; troubles will come. The difference between those who crumble and those who grow lies in how they respond to them. James is urging us to change our perspective: to see trouble not as a punishment or setback, but as a process. A process through which God refines us, strengthens us, and develops our endurance.

Troubles test our faith. They expose what we truly believe. When life is smooth, it's easy to say, But when you're faced with uncertainty, loss, or adversity, that's when your faith gets real. That's when endurance begins to grow. Every test of faith is like a workout for the soul. The more you endure, the stronger you become.

I have seen this play out in my lifetime and again. One vivid example was when I was on my way to write the New York Bar Exam. The bus I was on was stopped, and to my utter shock, I was pulled off, arrested, and taken to a detention centre in Rochester, New York. I was later released after they discovered it was a case of mistaken identity. I then had to find my way to Buffalo, New York, where the exam was being held. It was one of the most emotionally draining moments of my life. But in that moment, I didn't realise that my faith was being tested and my endurance was growing.

Through that ordeal, God was teaching me something – to trust Him even when I couldn't trace

Him. My faith was being refined, and my endurance was developing. I went ahead to write that exam, and by God's grace, I passed the New York Bar Exam on my first attempt as a foreign-trained attorney. I was later admitted to the New York State Bar. For many years, I never spoke about that experience because it felt too painful. But recently, God reminded me that the reason I went through that trouble was so I could tell the story, not as a story of pain, but as a testimony of His faithfulness.

Now, when I look back, I tell that story with great joy. Because I see what God was doing through it. He was shaping my character, strengthening my endurance, and preparing me for greater responsibilities. What looked like a setback was actually a setup for growth.

That's what James means when he says, *"Let endurance grow."* Don't fight the process. Don't try to rush out of the storm. Let your endurance develop, because when it does, you will emerge stronger, wiser, and more complete; lacking nothing. God uses our trials to make us whole.

So, when troubles come your way, don't panic. Pause and ask, *"Lord, what are You teaching me through this?"* Because hidden in every trial is an opportunity for transformation. And one day, you'll look back at that storm and say, *"Thank You, Lord, for that season,"* because it built something in you that comfort, success, or ease never could.

**Prayer**

**Heavenly Father, thank You for Your Word, which reminds us to count it all joy when we face trials of many kinds. Help us to see our troubles through the lens of faith, not fear. Teach us to trust You in the process, knowing that You are building endurance and character within us. When our faith is tested, strengthen us to stand firm. And when our endurance is fully developed, may we be complete and lacking nothing. Turn our pain into purpose, our trials into testimonies, and our endurance into joy. In Jesus' name, we pray. Amen.**

# VERSE 21
# 2 TIMOTHY 1:7

*For God has not given us a spirit of fear and timidity, but of power, love, and self-discipline.*

Another one of the most reassuring reminders in Scripture about the nature of the spirit that God has placed within every believer. It teaches us that fear and timidity are not from God; they are foreign spirits that attempt to invade our minds, steal our peace, and cripple our faith. When fear takes root, it limits our ability to walk in the fullness of God's purpose. It clouds judgment, weakens confidence, and paralyses action. But Paul's message to Timothy, and to all of us, is clear: this is not who we are.

God has not given us a spirit of fear. That alone tells us something powerful: fear is not merely an emotion; it is a spirit. It seeks to dwell in us, to take over our thoughts, and to direct our actions. But as believers, we are not host to fear. We are host to God's Spirit – the Holy Spirit – who brings with Him power, love, and self-discipline.

The *"spirit of power"* means divine enablement. It means that through God's Spirit, we have the strength to overcome what ordinary humans cannot. It gives us courage in moments of uncertainty, strength in weakness, and resilience in the face of adversity. This spirit reminds us that we are not operating on human power alone but on divine power, the same power that raised Christ from the dead.

The *"spirit of love"* balances the power. Power without love can be reckless, but power infused with love is transformative. Love helps us act with compassion even when we feel threatened or afraid. Love helps us forgive when it would be easier to retaliate. Love gives meaning to the power that God has placed within us. It ensures that our actions reflect His heart and not our fears.

The *"spirit of self-discipline"* (or sound mind) keeps everything aligned. It represents mental stability, calmness, and spiritual clarity. Fear thrives in chaos and confusion, but the Spirit of God brings order and peace to our minds. Through self-discipline, we can control our thoughts, our emotions, and our actions. We don't let fear dictate how we live; we let faith and wisdom guide us.

I have personally experienced the truth of this verse. I remember one particular moment on a flight when sudden, irrational fear gripped me. Thoughts began to flood my mind about the plane dropping from the sky. I could feel anxiety rising, my heart beating faster, my palms sweating. But deep down, I knew this fear was not normal; it wasn't of God. I began to pray, quietly at first, then more intently, declaring this very verse: *"God has not given me a spirit of fear, but of power, love, and self-discipline."* After a few minutes of persistent prayer, the fear lifted completely. Peace replaced panic. My mind cleared, and I was able to enjoy the rest of the flight. That moment was a reminder that Scripture is not theoretical; it is alive and active.

Whenever fear tries to invade your heart, remember this: you already possess the antidote. The Spirit of power, love, and self-discipline is already within you. You don't have to beg God to give it to you. You simply have to activate it. Speak it. Pray it. Declare it. Fear will flee because light and darkness cannot coexist in the same place.

**Prayer**

Heavenly Father, thank You for the assurance that You have not given me a spirit of fear or timidity. Thank You for giving me a spirit of power, love, and self-discipline. Whenever fear tries to take hold of my heart, remind me of who I am in You. Fill me afresh with courage and boldness to face every challenge before me. Let Your love perfect every area of my life where fear once dwelled, and give me the discipline to guard my thoughts and stay anchored in Your truth. In Jesus' name, I pray. Amen.

# VERSE 22
# EPHESIANS 2:10

*For we are God's masterpiece. He has created us anew in Christ Jesus, so we can do the good things he planned for us long ago.*

One of my favourite verses, especially during the period when I began seeking to understand my purpose in life. I remember printing it out and placing it on my office wall as a daily reminder that I am God's masterpiece. That word – masterpiece – is not an ordinary description. It speaks of something intentional, carefully designed, and full of value. When an artist creates a masterpiece, it's the best work they've ever produced. Every stroke, every colour, every detail is deliberate. That's how God views us – His finest creation, made in His image and crafted with purpose.

The verse continues to say, *"He has created us anew in Christ Jesus."* This means that our true identity and purpose come alive when we come into a relationship with Christ. In Him, we are made new. Whatever mistakes we made in the past, whatever limitations we once had, they no longer define us. God reshapes and renews us through Christ so that we can walk in the fullness of who we were always meant to be.

Then comes the most powerful part: *"so we can do the good things He planned for us long ago."* This means that our lives are not random or accidental. God already had a plan – a divine blueprint – for each of us. Long before we were born, He saw what we would become and the good works we would do. It's just like what God told Jeremiah in **Jeremiah 1:5:** *"Before I formed you in the womb I knew you; before you were born I set you apart; I appointed you as a prophet to the nations."* That verse echoes the same truth: God knew us, He designed us, and He assigned us a purpose before we even took our first breath.

When I meditate on this, it gives me confidence and clarity. I am not here by chance. My existence has meaning, my work has value, and my life fits into God's greater plan. Even when things don't make sense or when I feel inadequate, this verse reminds me that God didn't make a mistake when He made me. He took His time, and everything about me, my strengths, weaknesses, experiences, and even my scars are part of His masterpiece.

It's also a gentle challenge: if God created me anew in Christ for good works, then I must walk in them. It's not enough to know that I am a masterpiece; I must live out the purpose for which I was created. That purpose might be to inspire, to lead, to heal, to serve, or to create. But whatever it is, it is good because God planned it Himself.

When I understood this, I began to see purpose not as something I had to invent but as something I had to discover. My purpose was already written into the fabric of who I am. God simply invited me to walk in it each day.

**Prayer**

**Heavenly Father, thank You for reminding me that I am Your masterpiece. Thank You for taking the time to create me with purpose and love. Help me to see myself as You see me; fearfully and wonderfully made. Renew my mind daily in Christ Jesus so that I may walk in the good works You prepared for me long ago. Give me clarity to discern my purpose and courage to live it out fully. Let my life be a reflection of Your artistry and grace. In Jesus' name, Amen.**

# VERSE 23
# ISAIAH 49:26

*I will feed your enemies with their own flesh. They will be drunk with rivers of their own blood. All the world will know that I, the Lord, am your Savior and your Redeemer, the Mighty One of Israel.*

This is one of the dangerous verses in the Bible that someone can pray. I first heard it at an all-night service, and I remember thinking to myself, I need to read that again! The words were so striking that they stayed with me long after that night. Interestingly, I memorised it without even trying. Today, it still lives vividly in my memory. I even printed it out and pasted it on the wall in my office when I worked at Jubilee House. A few times when people walked in and saw that particular verse, they would pause, read it carefully, and then ask me what it meant. Some would simply nod quietly and leave. It paints a very scary picture indeed, but it also reveals something deep about the nature of God and how fiercely He protects His own.

At this point, we realize that God does not joke with those He intends to protect. He is a loving Father, but He is also a consuming fire. This verse is not about human vengeance or cruelty; it's about divine justice. When God decides to fight for you, He does it completely. He doesn't take half-measures. When you walk closely with Him, He becomes your Defender. And when the enemy rises against you, the Lord Himself takes up the battle. He doesn't need you to fight, He fights for you.

The imagery in this verse, *"feeding your enemies with their own flesh"* and *"drinking rivers of their own blood"*, is symbolic of complete self-destruction. It means those who plot evil against you will be consumed by the very traps they set for you. Those who dig a pit for you will fall into it themselves. It is a terrifying reminder that when God is on your side, no weapon formed against you shall prosper. Your enemies' plans will backfire; they will destroy themselves with their own schemes.

This verse also shows that when God acts, He does it publicly. It says, *"All the world will know that I, the Lord, am your Savior and your Redeemer."* In other words, your deliverance will be so visible that everyone around will recognise that it was the Lord who saved you. God wants His glory to be seen. When He vindicates you, it's not just to make you feel good. It's so that others will know that you serve the Mighty One of Israel.

I have personally seen moments in life when people underestimated the hand of God in my affairs. There were times when people plotted behind closed doors, thinking no one would ever know. Yet somehow, God exposed them and turned their own words against them. When you serve a living God, He ensures that your enemies become their own undoing.

So, when I remember this verse that was on my wall, I am reminded that I was never defenseless. It reminds me that I don't need to waste time fighting battles that belong to God. I simply need to stand still and watch Him act. He is both my Saviour and my Redeemer. He doesn't just save me from danger, He redeems my story, restores my peace, and ensures that His glory is revealed through my life.

**Prayer**

**Heavenly Father, Mighty One of Israel, thank You for being my Defender and my Redeemer. Thank You for fighting battles that I do not even see. Lord, I**

surrender every struggle and every enemy into Your hands. Fight for me, and let all the world know that You are my Saviour and my Redeemer. May those who plot evil against me fall into their own traps, and may Your glory be revealed in my deliverance. I rest in the assurance that no weapon formed against me shall prosper. In Jesus' name, Amen.

# VERSE 24
# EXODUS 14:14

*The Lord himself will fight for you. Just stay calm.*

This is one of those verses that demands you to pause and truly breathe. Imagine the God of old, the same God who parted the Red Sea, brought down the walls of Jericho, shut the mouths of lions, and silenced raging storms, stepping into battle for you. That is what this verse promises. It tells us that the Lord Himself, not an angel, not a prophet, not a friend, but the Lord Himself will fight for you. That in itself is enough to make you stand still in awe.

This verse was first spoken by Moses to the Israelites when they stood terrified at the edge of the Red Sea. Before them was the sea; behind them was Pharaoh and his mighty army, drawing closer by the minute. In human logic, it was a hopeless situation, trapped with no visible way out. But Moses, filled with divine authority, told them, *"The Lord himself will fight for you. Just stay calm."* It was as if he was saying, *"Do not panic. Do not run. Do not try to fix this by your own strength. Just stand firm and watch what God will do."*

That instruction to stay calm is often the hardest part. We live in a world that tells us to do something, to take control, to fight back, to defend ourselves. Yet God sometimes says, *"Be still."* Because He knows that in our stillness, we make room for Him to act. When we stop trying to fix everything ourselves, He steps in with power beyond human understanding.

I have seen this truth unfold in my own life. When I sat in that detention centre in Rochester, New York, unsure of what was happening or how long it would last, I remembered this verse. I had every reason to panic, but I chose to stay calm. I prayed and waited. For hours, nothing changed. But eventually, the truth came to light, and they realised they had made a mistake. I didn't have to argue or fight, God fought for me. Later, when I sat for that exam, I still carried the peace of that moment. It was as if God whispered, *"You see? I've got you."*

That is the beauty of this verse; when you've seen God fight for you once, your confidence in Him deepens. You begin to approach challenges differently. You no longer panic when things don't go your way. You don't waste time trying to explain yourself to everyone. You just stay calm. Because you know that the Lord Himself, the Creator of heaven and earth, is fighting on your behalf.

And the truth is, when God fights for you, He does so with precision. He knows every heart, every motive, every hidden conversation, and every unseen plot. He knows where to strike, when to move, and how to deliver you in a way that leaves others saying, *"Who is this person? How did they come out of that?"* It's because God showed up.

So, when life corners you between the *"Red Sea"* and *"Pharaoh's army,"* don't lose faith. Don't let fear dictate your next move. Let God handle the battle. Stay calm. Pray. Trust. And watch Him work.

**Prayer**

**Heavenly Father, thank You for being my defender and my warrior. Thank You for fighting battles that I cannot see and handling situations far beyond my understanding. Teach me to be still when everything in me wants to act. Help me to trust You completely, knowing that You will always fight for me. May Your peace fill my heart as I rest in Your power and timing. In Jesus' name, I pray. Amen.**

# VERSE 25
# EXODUS 23:25

*So you shall serve the Lord your God, and He will bless your bread and your water. And I will take sickness away from the midst of you.*

This verse is a covenant promise. It is both a call to service and a declaration of divine provision and protection. It reminds us that there are blessings attached to serving God faithfully.

When I think of this verse, I am reminded of the many times I have used it on Covenant Sundays together with **Genesis 17:1-2.** It's a verse that represents partnership, an agreement between you and God. You do your part – serve Him faithfully – and He does His part, blesses and protects you. Serving God here doesn't only mean working in the church or singing in the choir. It goes beyond that. It's about living a life that honours Him, seeking His will daily, and walking in obedience to His Word.

The promise that *"He will bless your bread and your*

*water"* is a powerful one. Bread and water symbolise the essentials of life; your food, your sustenance, and your daily needs. When God blesses them, they are multiplied, and lack is eliminated. It means God's blessing extends to your provision, ensuring that you always have what you need to survive and even thrive. It's the same principle seen when Jesus blessed the five loaves and two fish; the little became more than enough. When God's blessing rests on your bread and water, scarcity is replaced with abundance.

Then there's the second part: *"I will take sickness away from the midst of you."* God doesn't just stop at providing; He also preserves. Provision without health is incomplete. So, He makes a full promise: not only will He meet your physical needs, but He will also remove anything that seeks to destroy your well-being. This covers physical sickness, emotional affliction, and even spiritual weakness. It's God's way of saying, *"I will sustain you in every area of your life."*

In my own life, I have seen this verse come alive. Whenever I have renewed my covenant with God, whether at the start of a year or a new season, I have witnessed His faithfulness. There were times I felt worn out, yet I saw strength return. Times when provision seemed uncertain, yet everything I needed came through. That's the beauty of serving God. He never forgets those who are faithful to Him.

When you make a covenant with God, you're telling Him, *"Lord, I will serve You with all my heart, and I trust You to keep Your promise."* And He always does. His Word never fails.

**Prayer**

**Heavenly Father, thank You for this covenant promise. Thank You for reminding me that when I serve You faithfully, You bless my bread and my water and take sickness away from me. Lord, I renew my covenant with You today. Let Your blessings overflow in my life. Multiply my resources, strengthen my body, and preserve my health. May everything connected to me experience Your divine touch. I choose to serve You wholeheartedly, knowing that You are faithful to every promise. In Jesus' name, Amen.**

# VERSE 26
# JOSHUA 1:8

*This Book of the Law shall not depart from your mouth, but you shall meditate in it day and night, that you may observe to do according to all that is written in it. For then you will make your way prosperous, and then you will have good success.*

This verse is one of the foundational pillars for Christian living and personal growth. It was God's direct instruction to Joshua as he prepared to lead the Israelites into the Promised Land after Moses' death. Joshua faced a daunting task; leading a nation into battle, managing tribes with differing opinions, and filling the shoes of one of the greatest leaders in Israel's history. In the midst of that, God didn't give him a military strategy or political plan. Instead, He gave him a spiritual command: Stay rooted in My Word.

In today's world, this verse is still as relevant as ever. When God says, *"This Book of the Law shall not depart from your mouth,"* He is telling us that His

Word should be constantly on our lips. It's not something we only speak on Sundays or in church; it should shape our daily conversations, decisions, and actions. What we speak reflects what we believe, and when the Word of God fills our mouths, it also fills our hearts and minds.

The next instruction is powerful: "*You shall meditate in it day and night.*" Meditation here doesn't mean sitting quietly with our eyes closed; it means thinking deeply, reflecting, and allowing the Word to take root in our hearts. It's like marinating meat before cooking; the longer it sits in the seasoning, the deeper the flavour. In the same way, when we soak our minds in Scripture, it begins to transform our thoughts, words, and actions.

When I think of this verse, I remember growing up and hearing *people say someone "knew something by heart."* Those who knew their lessons by heart always excelled; they didn't just read the notes; they lived and breathed them. That's exactly what God is saying here. Knowing His Word *"by heart"* makes it part of your DNA. It shapes how you respond to life's challenges, how you treat people, and how you make decisions.

Then comes the next part: *"That you may observe to do according to all that is written in it."* The goal of reading and meditating is obedience. God's Word is for inspiration and instruction. We meditate not just to feel good but to do good. It's one thing to know Scripture; it's another to live it. When we start living the Word, we begin to experience the results of walking in God's divine principles.

And then comes the promise, *"For then you will make your way prosperous, and then you will have good success."* The phrase *"good success"* is so profound because it implies there is such a thing as bad success. Not all success is from God. You can succeed at the wrong thing, you can prosper in ways that destroy your peace, and you can win battles that cost you your soul. But good success, the kind God promises, comes with peace, joy, and purpose. It's success that aligns with His will, that uplifts others, and that brings glory to Him.

So, if you want to prosper and have good success in your career, family, health, and spiritual life, the formula hasn't changed: stay rooted in God's Word. Read it, speak it, meditate on it, and live it. Let the Bible guide your decisions. Let it be the standard by which you measure everything. When you do, your life aligns with divine order, and prosperity follows naturally; not just material prosperity, but wholeness in every area of your life.

**Prayer**

**Heavenly Father, thank You for Your Word that gives life and direction. Teach me to love and meditate on it day and night. Let it never depart from my mouth, but let it shape my thoughts, words, and actions. Help me to observe and obey everything written in it so that I may walk in Your will. Grant me not just success, but good success, success that honours You and blesses others. Prosper my way according to Your Word and let my life be a living testimony of Your faithfulness. In Jesus' mighty name, Amen.**

# VERSE 27
# JOSHUA 1:9

*Have I not commanded you? Be strong and of good courage; do not be afraid, nor be dismayed, for the Lord your God is with you wherever you go.*

One of the most reassuring commands God gives to His children. It's not just a suggestion – it's a command. God tells Joshua, and by extension all of us, to be strong and courageous. Why? Because He knows life will often present moments that test our strength and threaten our peace. Joshua was about to take over leadership from Moses and lead Israel into the Promised Land, a daunting task that could have easily overwhelmed him. But God didn't want fear or doubt to cripple him. Instead, He reminded Joshua that His presence would go with him wherever he went.

This verse reminds us that courage is not the absence of fear, but the decision to trust God in the middle of fear. God doesn't promise that we will never face challenges, uncertainty, or even opposition. What He

116

promises is His presence, and that changes everything. As believers, we can take comfort in knowing that God goes before us, stands beside us, and walks behind us.

In my own life, I've experienced moments when I needed this verse deeply; times I had to stand before powerful men, make difficult decisions, or take on responsibilities that felt too big for me. Each time, I whispered a simple prayer: *"Lord, help me to be strong and courageous. Let me speak only what You want me to say."* Just like Peter and John in **Acts 4,** who prayed for boldness before addressing the Sanhedrin, I found that God always supplied the courage I needed at the right time.

We can live confidently when we know that wherever we go — whether it's into a boardroom, courtroom, hospital room, or even an unfamiliar season of life — God is already there. He is with us wherever we go, guiding, protecting, and strengthening us.

So, the next time you feel afraid or uncertain, hear God's voice gently reminding you: *"Have I not commanded you? Be strong and of good courage."*

**Prayer**

Heavenly Father, thank You for Your constant presence in my life. When fear and doubt try to take hold of my heart, remind me of Your command to be strong and courageous. Help me to trust that You are with me wherever I go. Give me boldness to speak and act in faith, knowing that You will never leave nor forsake me. In Jesus' name, I pray. Amen.

# VERSE 28
# MALACHI 3:10

*"Bring all the tithes into the storehouse so there will be enough food in my Temple. If you do," says the Lord of Heaven's Armies, "I will open the windows of heaven for you. I will pour out a blessing so great you won't have enough room to take it in! Try it! Put me to the test!"*

This verse is one of the most direct and bold invitations from God in Scripture. It is the only place in the entire Bible where God Himself tells us to test Him. In most cases, we are warned not to test God, but here He gives us permission — almost a challenge — to prove His faithfulness in our giving. That alone tells us how serious and sacred the act of tithing is in our walk with God.

When I started working as a lawyer, I found it difficult to pay my tithe. I had heard about tithing but didn't think it was necessary or compulsory. Like many young professionals, I rationalised it. I argued that the money goes to the church, and pastors use it however they wish. I wanted accountability, figures, and reports. I thought I was being wise, but in truth, I was hiding behind logic to avoid obedience.

One Sunday, after church, as I drove home with my mother, we had a deep conversation about tithing. I made my arguments passionately, but my mother, calm, wise, and full of faith, spoke to me with gentleness. She told me something that completely shifted my mindset: *"Tithing is not about the church or the pastor. It is an act of faith between you and God."* That stuck with me. I went home reflecting on her words, and in my quiet time, I began to study the Scriptures about tithing. That's when I encountered this verse: **Malachi 3:10**, and the Holy Spirit opened my understanding.

I saw that tithing was not about losing money; it was about acknowledging that everything I have belongs to God. He gives us all, and in return, asks for a tenth; not because He needs it, but because He wants to see our trust. The tithe is a sign that we recognise Him as our source, our provider, and our sustainer. God doesn't need our money. He wants our obedience.

This verse also reveals something profound about God's character: He is both generous and faithful. He says, *"If you do, I will open the windows of heaven for you and pour out a blessing so great you won't have enough room to take it in."* That imagery is powerful. Picture the windows of heaven literally being opened over your life, blessings flowing in such abundance that they overflow into every area of your life: your health, your peace, your relationships, your career, and your purpose. God promises not just enough, but more than enough.

And then, the verse ends with that bold invitation, *"Try it! Put Me to the test."* This isn't arrogance on God's part; it's confidence in His own integrity. He knows that when we take a step of faith, He will never fail us. When I finally decided to obey and pay my tithe faithfully, I told God, *"Lord, I am taking You at Your Word."* And He proved Himself true. Doors began to open, opportunities I didn't apply for came my way, my finances stretched further than I thought possible, and I never lacked. It was as though the *"windows of heaven"* had truly been opened over my life.

Tithing has since become a sacred rhythm in my life, not out of compulsion, but out of gratitude and faith. It reminds me that God is my ultimate provider, not my salary, not my clients, not my position. Every time

I tithe, I'm saying, *"God, I trust You more than my income."* And every time, He responds with faithfulness.

So, if you've ever doubted whether tithing makes a difference, I encourage you to take God at His Word. *"Try it! Put Him to the test."* You will discover that obedience in giving opens spiritual and physical doors that no human effort could ever achieve.

**Prayer**

**Heavenly Father, thank You for being my source and my provider. Thank You for teaching me that tithing is not about money but about trust and obedience. Lord, help me to give faithfully and joyfully, knowing that everything I have belongs to You. Open the windows of heaven over my life and pour out blessings that I may be a blessing to others. Let my giving be an act of worship and a testimony of Your faithfulness. In Jesus' name, I pray. Amen.**

# VERSE 29
# ZECHARIAH 4:6

*So he answered and said to me: "This is the word of the Lord to Zerubbabel: 'Not by might nor by power, but by My Spirit,' says the Lord of hosts.*

This verse is about the true source of strength and success. It was spoken to Zerubbabel, the governor of Judah, who had the daunting task of rebuilding the temple after the Babylonian exile. The work ahead of him was enormous, resources were scarce, opposition was fierce, and morale was low. Yet, in the midst of all this, God sent this powerful word: *"Not by might nor by power, but by My Spirit."*

That statement alone shatters our human assumptions about success and achievement. It tells us that God's work cannot be accomplished through human effort alone. Our education, our connections, our resources, and even our wisdom – all of these have limits. But the Spirit of God knows no limits. When God's Spirit is at work, doors open that no human could ever open. Mountains move that no human strength could ever shift.

In our daily lives, we often rely heavily on our own abilities. We wake up, plan, strategise, execute, and sometimes even pray only as an afterthought. But this verse calls us to a higher dependence. It reminds us that the source of our success is not in our might or our power, not in our hustle or grind, but in God's Spirit.

When you pause and think about it, the Spirit of God is the same Spirit that hovered over the face of the deep in **Genesis 1:2** before creation began. It was that same Spirit who brought order out of chaos when God spoke the Word. That same Spirit empowered David to defeat Goliath, filled Solomon with wisdom, strengthened Elijah against false prophets, and descended upon Jesus at His baptism. That Spirit still works today; in our homes, our workplaces, our ministries, and even in the quiet battles of our hearts.

There have been times in my own life when I tried to do things solely on my own strength. I planned everything meticulously, prepared thoroughly, and executed perfectly, or so I thought. Yet things still didn't move. It was only when I stopped, prayed, and allowed the Holy Spirit to take control that I saw breakthroughs. It was as though the same plans suddenly came alive. That's when I truly understood what this verse means. The Spirit of God does not just help us; He enables us. He breathes life into what would otherwise remain lifeless.

When you face a mountain that looks impossible, remember that it will not move by your power or your intellect but by the Spirit of the Lord. When you are weary, when your strength is gone, when your might is exhausted, that's when the Spirit of God steps in. He does the impossible for God's glory.

So today, whatever task or challenge you face – whether in your family, your work, your calling, or your faith – let this verse echo in your heart: *"Not by might, nor by power, but by My Spirit,"* says the Lord of hosts.

**Prayer**

**Heavenly Father, thank You for reminding me that my strength and my power are limited, but Your Spirit knows no bounds. Teach me to depend not on my abilities but on Your Spirit. Breathe life into every plan, every dream, and every effort I place before You. Fill me afresh with Your Holy Spirit and let Your**

power work through me to accomplish what You have called me to do. May Your Spirit level every mountain before me, and may all glory return to You alone. In Jesus' name, I pray. Amen.

# VERSE 30
# ZECHARIAH 4:10

*Do not despise these small beginnings, for the Lord rejoices to see the work begin, to see the plumb line in Zerubbabel's hand.*

This verse is a beautiful reminder that God values process just as much as outcome. We live in a world that celebrates success, numbers, and visible impact, but God celebrates beginnings. He delights not in the finished building alone, but in the moment when the first stone is laid, the first prayer is said, the first seed is planted.

When I first discovered this verse, I thought to myself, wow. How often do we underestimate the power of starting small? We tend to think small beginnings are insignificant, unworthy of attention or applause. Yet, God's Word tells us not to despise them. He rejoices to see the work begin; to see faith taking its first step, to see obedience taking shape in motion.

I have seen this truth play out in my own life. When

we started our law firm, VINT & Aletheia, it was born in the study of our home. We had one client – just one. It would have been easy to think that wasn't much. But one client led to another, and another. Before long, we moved into an office space that my father graciously offered us. We hired a couple of young lawyers, began to train them, and grew together as a team. Fast forward to today, by God's grace, we have a whole administrative team, multiple lawyers, an office in New York, and recognition from international ranking entities. Looking back, I know that God rejoiced when He saw us start – when the plumb line was in our hands, even before the building took shape.

That's what this verse teaches: God rejoices in beginnings because they are acts of faith. They say, *"Lord, I trust You enough to start even when I can't see the end."* The world may measure success by how far you've gone, but Heaven measures it by the courage to begin.

So, whatever dream or idea God has placed in your heart, start. Don't despise the small beginnings. Start where you are, with what you have, and trust that God, who rejoices in your beginning, will bring it to completion.

**Prayer**

Heavenly Father, thank You for reminding me that You delight in small beginnings. Give me the faith to start, even when the path ahead is unclear. Teach me not to despise the days of little progress, but to trust that every small step matters to You. Bless the works of my hands, Lord, and let the things You have begun in me grow to bring You glory. In Jesus' name, Amen.

# VERSE 31
# LUKE 22:31-32

*And the Lord said, "Simon, Simon! Indeed, Satan has asked for you, that he may sift you as wheat. But I have prayed for you, that your faith should not fail; and when you have returned to Me, strengthen your brethren.*

This is one of those verses that grips your spirit the moment you hear it. I still remember exactly where I was when the Holy Spirit drew my attention to it. I was walking through Tangariro Square in Dumfries, Virginia, listening to a sermon by Pastor Rick Warren. As soon as I heard these words, I stopped in my tracks. It reminded me of the story of Job, how Satan asked God for permission to test him. The similarity was unmistakable. Here again, Satan had asked for permission to attack someone; this time, Peter. The language Jesus used was striking: *"Satan has asked for you, that he may sift you as wheat."*

What a sobering thought. Sifting wheat involves shaking, tossing, and separating. It's a process that removes impurities but is rough and unsettling. It means Peter was about to go through a season of shaking, a time of testing and breaking. And the shocking part is that Jesus didn't say, *"I stopped Satan."* He didn't say, *"I told him no."* He said instead, *"But I have prayed for you, that your faith should not fail."*

That was a revelation moment for me. It told me two powerful truths. Firstly, Jesus prays for us when we go through trials. We are not left alone in the storm. Even when it feels like everything is falling apart, the Son of God is interceding for us. Just as He told Peter, He tells us today, *"I have prayed for you."* That is the same Jesus who now sits at the right hand of the Father, making intercession for us daily **(Romans 8:34)**.

Secondly, Jesus' prayer is not that we avoid trials, but that our faith survives them. That was profound. I had always thought that if God loved me, He would protect me from trouble. But this verse turned that belief on its head. God's priority is not our comfort; it's our faith. He knows that trials refine us, just like gold in fire. The shaking may come, but His prayer is that our faith will not fail in the shaking. Indeed, **James 1:2-4** tells us that falling into various trials is a testing of our faith and that we should consider it a great joy.

We build our faith through these trials, and we become perfect and complete, lacking nothing.

When I reflected on this, I realised how intentional God is with our tests. Just like Peter, I too have been *"sifted."* One of the clearest examples was my detention experience in Rochester, New York. I could not understand why God would allow me to go through that. I prayed, questioned, and wrestled with the experience. But recently, the Lord reminded me that I went through that so that I could strengthen others with my testimony. That's the third lesson in this passage. Jesus told Peter, *"When you have returned to Me, strengthen your brethren."*

Every trial we endure is meant to be shared as a testimony. **Revelation 12:11** tells us that we overcome by the blood of the Lamb and by the word of our testimony. Our stories are weapons of encouragement. They remind others that if God could bring us through it, He can bring them through theirs. Sometimes, the reason God allows our sifting is so that someone else's faith can be strengthened when we testify of His goodness.

So yes, Satan may ask to sift us. God may even allow it. But we have an Advocate who prays for us, that our faith may stand firm. And when we emerge from the fire, our assignment is clear: *to go back and strengthen others.*

**Prayer**

**Lord Jesus, thank You for this powerful reminder that You intercede for us. Thank You for praying that our faith will never fail, even in the midst of trials and tribulations. When we go through seasons of sifting, help us to remember that You are with us and that Your prayer covers us. Strengthen our faith, Lord, and when we have overcome, teach us to return and strengthen our brethren with our testimonies. We ask that You continue to pray for us always, that our faith may endure until the end. In Your precious name we pray. Amen.**

# VERSE 32
# MARK 11:23-24

*For assuredly, I say to you, whoever says to this mountain, 'Be removed and be cast into the sea,' and does not doubt in his heart, but believes that those things he says will be done, he will have whatever he says. Therefore I say to you, whatever things you ask when you pray, believe that you receive them, and you will have them.*

My attention was first drawn to this verse by the late Kenneth Hagin, a man of deep faith whose teachings shaped generations of believers around the world. I remember getting every tape of his that I could find. I would play them over and over, sometimes even leaving them on through the night as I slept. There was something about the way he spoke about faith, not as an abstract concept but as a living, breathing force that connects us to God's power. This particular verse from the Gospel of Mark was one he often quoted, and it became one of the pillars of my spiritual journey.

Jesus here teaches us something profound: faith is not passive. It is not simply hoping that something might happen. Faith speaks. Faith acts. Faith declares. Jesus said, *"Whoever says to this mountain..."*, not whoever thinks about it or wishes it away, but whoever speaks to it. This shows us that faith must be voiced. There is power in the words we speak when they are rooted in belief.

Recently, while in Egypt with my family, we visited the Cave Church of St. Simon the Tanner in Cairo. The church itself is carved into a mountain and carries a remarkable story of faith. According to history, during the 10th century, a Muslim Caliph challenged the Christian community to prove the truth of their faith by literally moving a mountain; something that seemed humanly impossible. The Christians, led by a humble man named St. Simon the Tanner, fasted and prayed fervently for three days. On the final day, the story goes that as they prayed, the mountain shook and lifted, moving from its place. Whether one interprets this as literal or symbolic, the message is clear: faith in God can move what the world calls immovable.

In our modern times, our *"mountains"* may not be made of rock or sand. They may be financial struggles, health battles, broken relationships, emotional pain, or seemingly insurmountable obstacles at work or in life. Yet Jesus' promise still holds true: if we do not doubt in our hearts but believe that what we ask in prayer will come to pass, we will see it happen. The key lies in the heart and not in wishful thinking, but in unwavering belief.

**James 1:6–8** reminds us of this truth: *"But when you ask, you must believe and not doubt, because the one who doubts is like a wave of the sea, blown and tossed by the wind. That person should not expect to receive anything from the Lord."* Doubt is the enemy of faith. It weakens our confidence in God's promises and clouds our spiritual vision. But when we pray with conviction, believing that God hears us and that His promises are true, we set divine power in motion.

Faith doesn't mean we always see instant results. Sometimes God uses waiting to refine our hearts, strengthen our endurance, and align our desires with His will. But every prayer spoken in faith plants a seed. And in due season, it bears fruit.

**Prayer**

**Heavenly Father, thank You for reminding us through**

Your Word that with faith, all things are possible. Strengthen our faith, Lord, so that we may speak to the mountains in our lives with confidence and authority. Remove every trace of doubt and fear from our hearts. Help us to believe, even when we cannot see, and to trust that Your timing is perfect. May our prayers be filled with faith that moves mountains and hearts that rest in Your promises. In Jesus' mighty name, Amen.

# VERSE 33
# COLOSSIANS 3:23-24

*And whatever you do, do it heartily, as to the Lord
and not to men, knowing that from the Lord you
will receive the reward of the inheritance; for you
serve the Lord Christ.*

This verse from Paul's letter to the Colossians is one of
the most practical scriptures in the Bible for daily
living, especially in our work and professional life. It
reminds us that our ultimate supervisor is not our
boss, not our client, not our manager – but God
Himself. Whatever task we put our hands to, we are to
do it heartily, meaning with sincerity, diligence, and
passion, as though God were the one directly
assigning and reviewing it.

In my professional life and career, this verse has
served as a major guiding light. It has shaped how I
approach my work, regardless of who is watching or
how others behave. In Ghana, there's a common
saying, *"The job doesn't belong to my father,"* often
used to justify carelessness or mediocrity in the

workplace. It's a phrase that reveals a mindset of detachment, a belief that one can do the bare minimum because the work isn't personal. But for believers, **Colossians 3:23–24** calls us to a much higher standard. Our work is personal because we do it for the Lord.

When we shift our mindset from *"working for men"* to *"working for God,"* everything changes. We stop cutting corners. We stop complaining about who gets the credit. We stop being swayed by who notices and who doesn't. Instead, we begin to find meaning and purpose in even the most mundane tasks, because we recognise that our true reward doesn't come from a paycheck or human praise, but from the Lord Himself.

This perspective also protects us from bitterness and burnout. When we work only for human approval, we easily grow resentful or disillusioned. But when we see our work as worship, we find peace in knowing that God sees every effort, every late night, every extra step we take, even when no one else does.

I've found this truth deeply transformative. There were seasons when I struggled with imposter syndrome, feeling that I had to work extra hard to prove myself. But this verse reminded me that my effort was not about proving my worth to men but about honouring the One who had already called and equipped me. Whether I was writing a legal opinion, leading a team, or representing my country, I reminded myself: "*This is unto the Lord.*"

And there's a beautiful reciprocity in it; when we work as unto God, He elevates us before men. He opens doors no human could open and ensures that our reward, both here and eternally, comes from His own hand.

**Prayer**

**Lord Jesus, thank You for the reminder that whatever I do, I do it for You. Help me to work heartily, with diligence, humility, and excellence, not for the praise of men, but to honour You. Teach me to see my work as an act of worship and service to You. Deliver me from laziness, pride, or fear, and let my labour reflect Your glory. May my diligence inspire others, and may I always remember that my true reward comes from You, my Lord and Master. Amen.**

# VERSE 34
# 1 THESSALONIANS 5:18

*In everything give thanks; for this is the will of God in Christ Jesus for you.*

This verse is one of those simple yet deeply challenging instructions in the Bible. It sounds easy on the surface — *"in everything give thanks"* — but when life throws us unexpected challenges, disappointments, or pain, it becomes one of the hardest things to practice. Yet, it is exactly in those moments that this verse calls us to a higher level of faith and perspective.

When the Bible says, *"in everything"*, it does not say *"for everything."* There's a difference. We are not being told to give thanks for tragedy, sickness, betrayal, or loss — but to give thanks in those circumstances. Because even in the midst of hardship, God is still working. Even in the darkest hour, His presence has not left us. Gratitude becomes an act of faith, a declaration that we believe God is still sovereign and that something good can come out of what seems terrible.

I have heard this verse quoted many times at funerals or in times of grief, and indeed, it takes spiritual maturity to genuinely give thanks when you've lost something or someone dear. But I've also come to learn that thanksgiving is not only about expressing joy; it's about acknowledging trust. When we give thanks in the middle of uncertainty, we are essentially saying, *"Lord, I don't understand this, but I trust You."*

There have been moments in my own life where this verse was all I had to hold onto. When things didn't go as planned, when I faced closed doors or disappointments, I would remind myself that gratitude repositions the heart. It shifts your focus from what's missing to what's present, from despair to hope, from frustration to faith. Gratitude brings perspective.

The Bible says this is *"the will of God in Christ Jesus for you."* That means thanksgiving isn't just a suggestion — it's a divine directive. It is God's will because He knows that gratitude protects our hearts from bitterness and unbelief. When we live with a thankful heart, we stay aligned with God's purpose and keep our spiritual vision clear.

So, whether you are celebrating a victory or enduring a valley season, choose gratitude. It doesn't mean pretending everything is fine; it means trusting that God is at work, even when you can't see it, and thanking Him for it.

**Prayer**

**Heavenly Father, thank You for reminding me to give thanks in all things. Teach me to cultivate a heart of gratitude, not only in moments of joy but also in times of difficulty. Help me to trust that You are working all things together for my good. Let thanksgiving be my constant language and my posture of faith, no matter what season I find myself in. I choose to thank You today, for You are faithful, and Your mercy endures forever. In Jesus' name, Amen.**

# VERSE 35
# EPHESIANS 3:20

*Now to Him who is able to do exceedingly abundantly above all that we ask or think, according to the power that works in us.*

One of the most powerful declarations in the Bible about the limitless nature of God's ability. It begins with an affirmation: *"Now to Him who is able."* It reminds us that God is not just capable of answering prayers; He is able to exceed our wildest expectations. It's not just that He can do what we ask, He can do far more, exceedingly abundantly above all that we could ever ask, imagine, or even dream.

Simply put, God can blow your mind.

We often put limits on what God can do, not because He is limited, but because our faith is. We ask for things within the scope of what we think is possible, forgetting that we serve a God who specialises in impossibilities. He created the universe out of nothing, parted the Red Sea, raised the dead, and still works miracles in our everyday lives.

This verse is usually said as part of a blessing, but if we pause to meditate on it, it's a powerful statement of faith. It tells us that God's power is not only external, but it is also within us. The phrase *"according to the power that works in us"* means that God channels His ability through the faith, obedience, and willingness of His people. The Holy Spirit is that power within us, enabling us to do things that in our natural selves we could never accomplish.

I've seen this verse come alive in my own life. When my wife, Lady-Ann, first told me about her desire to advocate for mental health through the Wholesome Mind initiative, I thought to myself, *"This is enormous"*. The vision was vast — awareness campaigns, advocacy, education, and national impact. It seemed like something far bigger than us. But around that same time, the Holy Spirit whispered to me, *"Yes, it might be big to you, but it is nothing compared to what God can do."* And that has proven true. Every step of the journey has been marked by divine provision, open doors, and unexpected favour. It has been nothing short of exceedingly abundantly above all that we ask or think.

As Christians, we must learn to stop limiting God with our expectations. If our prayers are small, our faith may be too confined. But when we trust in His power working in us, we begin to see His greatness unfold. God is not intimidated by big dreams; He delights in them. So, dream boldly, pray fervently, and believe deeply. God's capacity is beyond human measure.

**Prayer**

**Heavenly Father, we thank You that You are able to do exceedingly abundantly above all that we ask or think. Thank You for reminding us that Your power is at work within us. Lord, expand our faith, stretch our imagination, and help us to trust You without limits. In every area of our lives — our families, careers, ministries, and dreams — do far beyond what we can conceive. Let Your power in us produce wonders for Your glory. In Jesus' mighty name, Amen.**

# VERSE 36
# PSALM 119:11

*Thy word have I hid in mine heart, that I might not sin against thee.*

This is one of those verses that has stayed with me since childhood. I remember memorising it during Sunday School, reciting it with ease in memory-verse competitions, and hearing it quoted by older Christians who always seemed to speak with deep conviction. At the time, I didn't fully understand the weight of it. I thought it simply meant that I should memorise Bible verses. But as I have grown in faith and experience, I have come to realise that this verse is much deeper. It's about making God's Word a permanent resident in our hearts.

When David said, *"Thy word have I hid in mine heart,"* he was not just talking about mental storage. He was talking about spiritual habitation. The Word of God was not merely something he remembered; it was something that shaped his thoughts, guided his decisions, and directed his behaviour. To *"hide"* the Word in one's heart means to internalise it so deeply that it becomes part of who you are. It's like a seed that takes root within your soul, bearing fruit in every situation.

There's also a practical wisdom in this verse. David understood the connection between God's Word and purity. He says, *"that I might not sin against thee."* When we hide the Word in our hearts, it acts as a spiritual compass that keeps us aligned with God's will. When temptation arises, the Word in our heart rises louder than the voice of sin. That's why Jesus Himself, when tempted in the wilderness, responded to Satan with Scripture. The Word He had hidden in His heart was His weapon of defense.

This verse beautifully connects to Joshua 1:8, which says, *"This Book of the Law shall not depart from your mouth, but you shall meditate in it day and night..."* The two verses are like twins of spiritual discipline. Joshua tells us to meditate on the Word continually; David tells us to hide it in our hearts. Joshua shows us the process; David shows us the outcome. When we meditate on God's Word day and night, it moves from our mind to our heart. Once it's in our hearts, it guides us away from sin and toward righteousness.

In my own life, I've found that the Word of God hidden in my heart often speaks to me in moments I least expect. When I am about to take a wrong step, the Holy Spirit brings a verse to mind. When I am discouraged, a hidden promise gives me strength. When I am uncertain, a Word I once read and tucked away suddenly becomes light to my path. That's why I've learned not just to read Scripture, but to treasure it, to make it my inner voice of wisdom and conviction.

The world we live in today bombards us with all kinds of noise, opinions, temptations, and distractions. The only way to remain steady is to have God's Word hidden within. Because when the noise grows loud, the hidden Word whispers truth, and that truth keeps us anchored.

**Prayer**

**Heavenly Father, thank You for Your Word that is living and powerful. Help me to hide it deep within my heart so that it becomes my guide, my comfort, and my defence. Teach me to meditate on it day and night and let it shape my thoughts and actions. When temptation comes, remind me of what You have said. When I am weary, let Your**

Word strengthen me. And when I am lost, let it lead me back to You. May Your Word not depart from my mouth nor my heart, that I may walk in Your ways all the days of my life. In Jesus' name, Amen.

# VERSE 37
# PSALM 119:105

*Thy word is a lamp unto my feet, and a light unto my path.*

Another powerful verse from **Psalm 119** — one that has shaped the faith of many since childhood. I remember this verse so vividly from the Scripture Union camps we attended as children. Those camps were special moments in my spiritual journey. We would pack our Bibles, notebooks, and the Daily Power devotionals, and gather with other children from across the country. Every morning began with songs, memory verses, and Bible competitions. This particular verse was a regular feature — one we recited so often that it became part of us. I can still remember the echo of dozens of young voices saying in unison, *"Thy word is a lamp unto my feet, and a light unto my path."*

It's a simple verse, but deeply insightful. It paints a picture of a traveller walking through a dark world. Without light, every step is uncertain. You could stumble, trip, or lose your way entirely. But when you carry a lamp, you can see where to place your feet and discern the right path ahead. That's exactly what God's Word does for us. Life's path is full of uncertainty, choices, challenges, temptations, and distractions, and without the Word of God, it's easy to lose direction.

When we read and meditate on Scripture, it becomes like a lamp to our feet, guiding our immediate steps, and a light to our path, showing us the broader direction of our lives. The Word helps us navigate both the now and the next. It gives clarity in confusion, hope in despair, and direction when the way forward seems foggy and unclear.

There have been moments in my life when I was unsure what decision to make — whether professionally, personally, or spiritually — and in those moments, the Word of God provided the light I needed. Sometimes it was a verse that came to mind at just the right time. Other times, it was a passage that reaffirmed God's presence and purpose in my life. That is what the Word does; it illuminates the darkness around us and within us, allowing us to walk with confidence, not fear.

The beautiful thing about light is that it doesn't remove the night; it helps you move through it. God's Word doesn't promise to remove all of life's difficulties, but it ensures that even in darkness, you will not be lost because you have His light to guide you.

**Prayer**

**Heavenly Father, thank You for Your Word that lights our path and guides our steps. In a world filled with confusion and darkness, may Your Word continually shine upon us. Help us to walk according to Your truth, to trust in Your promises, and to depend on Your guidance daily. Let Your Word dwell richly in our hearts so that we may never stumble but walk boldly in the light of Your wisdom. In Jesus' name, Amen.**

# VERSE 38
# LAMENTATIONS 3:22-23

*It is of the Lord's mercies that we are not consumed, because his compassions fail not. They are new every morning: great is thy faithfulness.*

This verse has always meant a lot to me. I remember first truly connecting with it because of CeCe Winans' song *"Great Is Thy Faithfulness"* from her album *"Alone in His Presence."* I still remember that morning vividly — we were on vacation in the United States, and my aunt, Mary Ofosu Adams (whom we all affectionately called Sister Aba), gathered us into her van as we drove from York, Pennsylvania to New York City to visit another aunt. The drive was about four hours long, and that album played throughout the entire journey. It was early morning, quiet, peaceful, and the music filled the car with such a sweet sense of God's presence. I didn't know it then, but later I discovered that the song was based on this verse from Lamentations — and it all made sense. The first stanza of the song is as follows:

*Great is Thy faithfulness, O God my Father*
*There is no shadow of turning with Thee*
*Thou changest not, Thy compassions, they fail not*
*As Thou hast been, Thou forever will be*
*Great is Thy faithfulness*
*Great is Thy faithfulness*
*Morning by morning new mercies I see*
*All I have needed Thy hand hath provided*
*Great is Thy faithfulness, Lord, unto me*

This verse reminds me that it's only by the Lord's mercy that we are not consumed — not by life's challenges, not by the plans of the enemy, and not by the weight of our own mistakes. There are so many moments in life when, looking back, I realise that if it weren't for God's mercy, I wouldn't have made it through. His compassion never fails, even when everything else does. Every single morning, He renews His mercy. That means every day is a fresh start, a new opportunity, another chance to see His hand at work.

What I love most about this verse is that it doesn't depend on our circumstances. It depends on who God is. His faithfulness doesn't change when we face difficulties. His mercy doesn't dry up when we fall short. Just as I remember that long, peaceful drive filled with worship and gratitude, I'm reminded that God's faithfulness accompanies us wherever we go.

To this day, *"Alone in His Presence"* remains one of my favourite albums. Whenever I need to draw closer to God or peace in my spirit, I put it on. It brings me back to that truth, that His compassions never fail, they are new every morning, and great indeed is His faithfulness.

**Prayer**

**Heavenly Father, thank You for Your unending mercy and compassion. Thank You that I am not consumed by the challenges of life because You renew Your mercy toward me every morning. Help me to always remember that no matter what I face, Your faithfulness never changes. Let each new day be a reminder of Your love, Your goodness, and Your grace. Great is Your faithfulness, Lord. Amen.**

# VERSE 39
# 2 CORINTHIANS 9:7-8

*You must each decide in your heart how much to give. And don't give reluctantly or in response to pressure. "For God loves a person who gives cheerfully." And God will generously provide all you need. Then you will always have everything you need and plenty left over to share with others.*

I first paid close attention to this verse and the ones that follow when I was preparing to share the Word of God with a church in Kumasi. Interestingly, I was not going to speak about giving. My message that day was meant to focus on faith, but this verse came alive in my spirit as I read it. The Holy Spirit illuminated it to me in a way I could not ignore. Even though it wasn't the subject of my sermon that day, I would later find myself returning to it over and over, allowing the Holy Spirit to teach me deeper truths about giving.

What I came to understand is that giving is truly an act of faith. When you give, especially when you give cheerfully, you are expressing trust in God as your source. It takes faith to release something valuable — your money, time, or resources — believing that God will not only replenish but multiply it. This verse makes a profound connection between giving and divine provision: *"And God will generously provide all you need."* That means when you give, you don't lose. You actually open the door for God to supply you with all you need, and more.

The part that blesses me most is that God doesn't just give back what you gave, He gives you everything you need and then adds plenty left over to share with others. This reveals God's heart for generosity: He blesses you not just for your sake but so that you can bless others. You become a channel, a pipe through which God's resources flow to meet the needs of people around you. The more He can trust you to give, the more He entrusts to you.

I remember reading further down in verse 14, and it struck me deeply, *"And they will pray for you with deep affection because of the overflowing grace God has given you."* That is powerful. When we give, we don't just bless people materially; we touch their hearts. Their response, *"God bless you,"* is more than a casual phrase. It is a prayer that ascends before God, and He honours it. Those prayers become seeds of blessing that come back to water your life.

In my personal walk with God, another verse that aligns perfectly with this is **Proverbs 3:28 (NLT)**: *"If you can help your neighbor now, don't say, 'Come back tomorrow, and then I'll help you.'"*

That verse has shaped my attitude towards giving. Whenever someone asks me for something and I have the means, I don't delay. I've learned not to overthink it or make excuses. Sometimes people may take advantage of it, yes, but I do it in obedience to God's command and out of love. My giving is between me and God, not me and man.

Over time, I have seen how God honours cheerful giving. He never allows a cheerful giver to lack. There have been moments in my life where I gave out of very little, only to see God multiply it back in ways I could never have planned. Giving truly draws you closer to the heart of God because God Himself is the ultimate Giver.

**Prayer**

**Heavenly Father, thank You for teaching me the beauty and power of cheerful giving. Thank You for**

providing all my needs and making me a vessel of Your generosity. Lord, continue to make me generous — generous with my resources, my time, my love, and my compassion. Help me to give freely and cheerfully, not reluctantly or out of pressure, but from a heart that trusts You completely. Let my giving bring glory to Your name and blessings to others. And may Your overflowing grace abound in my life always. In Jesus' name, Amen.

# VERSE 40
# ROMANS 10:17

*So faith comes from hearing, that is, hearing the*
*Good News about Christ.*

It is interesting that I end this book with this verse when, in fact, it is one of the verses that triggered my spiritual walk with Jesus Christ. I remember vividly my time at the Holy Trinity Resort and Spa at Sogakope, a time of solitude and deep reflection. I had gone there to pray and to seek clarity about my life. I wanted direction, purpose, and peace. And in that quiet place, God spoke to me and said, "Seek Me and My righteousness." That divine instruction changed everything.

While at Sogakope, I began to listen to one of the videos I had downloaded from YouTube to use during my retreat. It was a sermon by Bishop Dag Heward-Mills. In that sermon, he quoted this very verse, **Romans 10:17**, several times. Each time he repeated it, it sank deeper into my spirit: "*Faith comes by hearing, and hearing by the Word of* God." It reminded me of how Kenneth Hagin, too, used to dwell on this verse in his teachings on faith. That repetition was not just a coincidence; it was divine emphasis. God was calling my attention to something fundamental.

This verse teaches us something profound: faith does not come by accident. It is built, nurtured, and strengthened through a deliberate encounter with the Word of God. The more we hear the Good News, the more our faith grows. The more we fill our hearts with the Word, the less room there is for doubt. Just as our physical bodies are nourished by food, our spirits are nourished by the Word of God. Without hearing, there is no faith. Without faith, there is no power.

I began to understand that hearing was not a one-time act. It was a continuous process. Every day, we must tune our hearts to God's frequency through Scripture, worship, teaching, and fellowship with other believers. Each moment we spend hearing the Good News strengthens our faith for the next challenge, the next season, the next assignment.

As I look back on my journey, I realise how this single verse has been the bedrock of my growth in Christ. It is hearing that leads to believing, believing that leads to faith, and faith that leads to transformation. And so, it is only fitting that this verse closes this book because everything begins and ends with faith. Faith is the currency of our walk with God. Without it, we cannot please Him. But through it, we can move mountains, walk through storms, and live lives anchored in His Word.

**Final Prayer**

**Heavenly Father, thank You for Your Word that gives life, light, and faith. Thank You for every lesson, revelation, and moment of reflection throughout this journey. As I conclude this book, I pray that Your Word will continue to dwell richly in me and in everyone who reads these pages. May faith rise in our hearts each time we hear Your Good News. Let Your Word be the foundation upon which we build our lives, our families, and our futures. Strengthen our faith to trust You in all things and to walk boldly in the purposes You have set before us. May our hearts remain ever anchored in You and in Your Word.**

*In Jesus' mighty name,*
*Amen.*

# SPECIAL MESSAGES ON MY 40TH BIRTHDAY

I would like, at this moment, as you gather to celebrate the life of my younger brother and friend, Kow Abaka Essuman, to bring him the best of wishes in life. Kow Abaka Essuman, at this young age, you have achieved a lot. God has blessed you with wisdom and intellect. You come from a very Christian and wonderful family, and so you have the world at your feet. And God has been gracious. Everyone who loves you can see it. But I, in particular, enjoy the warmth and the joy with which you come to friendship. It is never lost on me that even when you were working in the Jubilee House, you made time to respond to messages, at least speaking for myself, you picked calls, and occasionally you got in touch. I was very, very impressed by that. I would like to carry forward in life that kind of spirit of engagement and warmth and be a blessing to your generation. I pray that the God who has brought you this far will carry forward the dreams that He has put in your heart. You will continue to be not just a citizen of this country but a world citizen, bringing your gifts, your abilities, your talents to bear on any situation in which you are called to serve. But in doing that, I would like to remind you that there may be pitfalls along the road. I pray that God will protect you, deliver you from evil, lead you away from temptation and help you to keep your focus. Keep your vision for life. Continue to be godly, and I believe that the God and Father of our Lord Jesus Christ, by the power of His spirit at work in you, will do the rest. I wish you a blessed and happy birthday, and may this birthday be a turning point marking greater things to come in your life and ministry. I wish you well. I wish you long life. I wish you every blessing in Christ, and I know that we will continue to rejoice in the triumphs of your life. God bless you. Be happy. Enjoy, and be a blessing to others. Happy Birthday. – **Most Rev. Johnson K. Asamoah-Gyadu, Presiding Bishop of the Methodist Church Ghana**

My Dearest Friend and Husband,

As we celebrate forty years of love, partnership, and purpose, I can confidently say that your life is a beautiful reflection of God's favour, presence, and faithfulness. Walking this journey with you has been one of my greatest blessings.

Your steadfast leadership and obedience to God have shaped our family and inspired everyone who knows you. You are a loyal friend, an incredible husband, and a loving father – a true role model and a light to our generation.

May this new chapter unfold even greater joy, wisdom, and fulfilment of your divine purpose. I thank God every day for the gift of you.

With all my love,

**Your wife, Lady-Ann Essuman**

**Special Birthday Wish to our Firstborn**

Today, November 7, 2025, our beloved son, **Kow Abaka Essuman, Esq.,** turns forty. As parents, we thank God for the gift of his life and the remarkable journey that has brought him this far. From his early years, Kow has shown determination, discipline, and a deep sense of purpose; qualities that continue to guide his life and work.

We are immensely proud of the man he has become: a devoted husband and father, a trusted professional, and a compassionate leader who serves with humility and integrity. Above all, Kow's faith in God remains his anchor and source of strength.

As he celebrates this milestone, our hearts overflow with gratitude for his life, his achievements, and the many ways God continues to use him to touch lives and make a difference.

With love and thanksgiving to God,

Your proud parents

**Ato & Sally Essuman**

Indeed, God has been faithful! Happy 40th birthday, big bro! May the Lord continue to guide you over the next 40 years so that you will be like a well-watered garden, like an ever-flowing spring to the family and the world at large. Stay blessed. Regards, **Nana Kow Appiah Essuman (Brother)**

4 decades of God's faithfulness, we celebrate and give thanks! Praying for the next 40 to be filled with everlasting love, grace, and peace! – **Kow Mensah Akaa Essuman, M.D. PhD (Brother)**

Kow is one of the most humble, kind and knowledgeable people I've come across and I am proud to have him as my eldest brother. On his 40th birthday, I would like to wish him the very best and may he continue to trust in the Lord in all he does and be a role model for many young minds across the world! – **Nana Yaw Atiapa Essuman (Brother)**

Happy Birthday Bro! Indeed God is a good God. I have been privileged to see God at work in your life and on this special occasion, I pray that God grants you more of all that you require to be a blessing and a credit to the kingdom of God. May God help you establish a lasting legacy which will be a testament to His Glory. Amen. – **Michelle Nana Yaa Essuman (née Ansah) (Sister-in-Law)**

Wishing a very happy birthday to a truly remarkable man – a distinguished attorney whose integrity, grit, and dedication set the highest standard. Your sharp mind, unwavering principles, and vibrant spirit inspire everyone lucky enough to know you. May this year bring you continued success, good health, and moments or well-earned joy. Keep shining in the courtroom and in life. You make excellence look effortless. Cheers to you and all that you are! – **Josephine Essuman, PhD (née Garban) (Sister-in-Law)**

As a God-brother by divine appointment, I have seen my brother Kow grow into a handsome, affable and courageous man. And above all, the Lord is with him! Thank God for bringing you this far with His divine guidance, goodness and favour. Happy Birthday. – **Isaac Kwamina Eshun Annan, PhD (Uncle/Brother)**

Kow is more than a brother-in-law; he's truly family. His humility and quiet strength have a way of touching everyone around him. Seeing the man he's become and the beautiful life he's built with my sister fills me with so much pride and admiration. Happy 40th to an amazing brother and friend. – **Genevieve Awo Alatise (née Krofah) (Sister-in-Law)**

Happy 40th, my friend and brother. You've always had this rare way of being completely yourself, honest, grounded, and true to what you believe in. That's what makes you who you are, and I hope you never change. I care about you and I'm really proud of the person you are! – **Olive Krofah (Sister-in-Law)**

Happy 40th Kow!!! You've built a life filled with purpose and meaning over the years and I believe the years ahead will be rewarding. Cheers to good health, new adventures and endless laughter with the people who love you. – **Lucy Atiapa Amanor (née Adams) (Cousin)**

You've had such a profound impact on my life, both directly and indirectly, and I'm forever grateful for following your lead which helped me find my path. May you always have the upper hand in life and remain abundantly blessed as countless as the sands on the shore. – **Opare Adams (Cousin)**

Abaka, your journey embodies grace and conviction, inspiring all who know you. May your 40th year unfold with renewed purpose and peace. – **Joseph Bernard Ashalley (Friend)**

Kow is now well known as Legal Counsel of former President Nana Akufo-Addo. As glowing as that is … I vividly remember a picture of Kow holding the President's worn-out sneakers at the end of a gruelling campaign trail. This was a man who had 3 law degrees from 3 continents by the age of 25. To me, it showed Kow's humility, faith, and commitment to the cause even if it meant him forgoing a glamorous position. Happy birthday Kow. God bless you and expand your territory. – **Fred Mawuli Deegbe, Jnr. (Friend)**

Abaka, I always smile a little harder when your name is mentioned and that's because I am ever so proud of you. I have watched you grow from the boy who would always defend my corner in college to the man whose name gets me into rooms of excellence. As you turn 40, I pray that you continue to be blessed and your household continues to bask in the favour of the Lord. As I thought of what to write, this verse instinctively jumped at me and I pray that you will continue to stand before kings. *"Seest thou a man diligent in his business? He shall stand before kings; He shall not stand before mean men."* – **Proverbs 22:29** KJV. Happy Birthday, Abaka. Love, Your twin **(Edyth)**

My brother Kow, I am glad and excited about your birthday. I welcome you to the fourth level! I really thank God for your life and how far He has brought you. One thing I have always said is that *"I am proud of you"* and I genuinely mean this from the bottom of my heart. Honestly, people walk into your life as classmates and end up becoming family. You, Kow, my good friend from school has been that person. Someone who started as just another face in the crowd but quickly became a brother for life. We've shared laughs, struggles, dreams, presentations, debates and countless memories that shaped who we are today. No matter where life takes us, I know that bond will never fade. Here's to a friendship that has turned into brotherhood which is built on loyalty, laughter, and years of unbreakable trust. Have a blessed birthday. – **Joel Odartey Lamptey (Friend)**

Happy 40th birthday to you my dear friend Kow! I'm grateful to call you my friend. I am so proud of you and everything that you have achieved! I will forever cherish all of our great memories at law school – what a year! So many jokes, so much stress, but we did it! The Caribbean connection (and Ghana!) Lots of Love always, **Davena (Friend)**

You have always walked your talk, and that is something I deeply admire about you bro. Your unwavering faith, kindness, and love for Christ speak more powerfully than any sermon. Long before we even knew ourselves, our families were connected, and I am grateful that this bond has blossomed into a genuine brotherhood. Keep shining, my brother. The world truly needs more hearts like yours. Happy 40th Birthday! May this new chapter usher in even greater grace, divide wisdom and influence as you continue to walk boldly in purpose and faith. *"Let your light so shine before men, that they may see your good works and glorify your Father in heaven."* – **Matthew 5:16** (NKJV). May you continue to shine even brighter to the glory of God even as you embark on this new chapter. – **Joel Vanderpuye (Friend)**

I met Kow twenty-three years ago, and we are more than brothers now. He is God-fearing, loyal, and trusted. I am not so surprised about his heights in politics and governance. We thank God for his life, and may He grant his highest ambition. Welcome to the fourth floor. – **Eugene Owusu-Asamoah (Friend)**

It is rare to find an individual whose character remains unwavering as they achieve success. Kow Abaka Essuman is that exception. His influence serves to elevate all those in his circle. Wishing you a wonderful birthday, Kow. May the coming year bring greater opportunities for you to inspire. – **Vijay Manu (Friend)**

# SIGNIFICANT MILESTONES – MY JOURNEY SO FAR

- Pioneering student of Alpha Beta School, Accra, Ghana.
- Attended Morning Star School, Cantonments, Accra, Ghana.
- Attended Prempeh College, Kumasi, Ghana.
- Attended Holborn College, London, U.K. and was awarded the Best Student Prize in Criminal Law.
- Attended the University of Westminster, London, U.K. and graduated with an Upper Second Class Bachelor of Laws degree. At Westminster, he was selected for a mini pupillage at Tooks Chambers, where he demonstrated a passion for the Bar.
- Accepted as a Student Barrister at the Honourable Society of Lincoln's Inn.
- Attended BPP Law School, London, U.K. and completed the Bar Vocational Course with a grade of Very Competent.
- Volunteered for the Free Representation Unit at the Royal Courts of Justice, London, U.K.
- Called to the Bar of England and Wales by the Honourable Society of Lincoln's Inn as a Barrister at Law.
- Attended Cornell Law School, Ithaca, New York,

- U.S.A and graduated with a Master of Laws degree with Honors in International Mergers and Acquisitions and Financial Institutions.
- Through the Public Interest Clinic at Cornell Law School, represented pro bono clients before the Unemployment Insurance Board and the Social Security Administration in New York. He won all cases.
- Sat and passed the New York Bar Exam on a first attempt as a foreign attorney.
- Admitted to the New York State Bar as an Attorney and Counselor-at-Law.
- Worked for law firms in London, representing clients before the Immigration Tribunals.
- Returned to Ghana and joined Reindorf Chambers, Accra
- Attended Ghana School of Law as a Post Call Law Course student.
- Admitted to the Ghana Bar as a Barrister and Solicitor of the Supreme Court of Ghana.
- Joined Bentsi-Enchill, Letsa and Ankomah and rose to the position of Senior Associate. He was described by a Supreme Court judge as a "rising advocate".
- Attended a Lex Mundi Institute Cross-Border Dispute Resolution Programme in Monterey, California, U.S.A.

- Selected as a Global Shaper of the World Economic Forum as a member of the Accra Hub. He was selected as one of 80 Africans to represent the Community at the Regional Meeting of the World Economic Forum in Cape Town. Co-authored a book with other Global Shapers.
- Served as Social Media Manager for Nana Addo Dankwa Akufo-Addo and New Patriotic Party from 2008 – 2024.
- Appointed Legal Counsel to the President of Ghana, Nana Addo Dankwa Akufo-Addo.
- Appointed twice as a member of the Constitutional and Legal Committee of the National Council of the New Patriotic Party
- Part-time lecturer at Zenith University College and Ghana School of Law.
- Appointed to the governing boards of State Interests and Governance Authority and Minerals Income Investment Fund.
- Attended the Blavatnik School of Government, University of Oxford, Oxford, U.K. and completed and Executive Education Programme on Oil, Gas and Mining Governance
- Completed an Executive Education programme on Negotiation and Leadership at the Harvard Law School, Cambridge, Massachusetts, U.S.A.

- Featured in a number of publication nd rankings including the front page of the Business and Financial Times, The Africa Report, Future of Ghana Top 30 under 30, Ghana's top 10 Inspirational Professional Executives under 40 by Glitz Africa, Most Influential Young Ghanaian, 100 Most Influential Young Africans, and 100 Most Influential People of African Descent.
- Recipient of the Honorary Award of the Head of State Scheme (The Duke of Edinburgh's International Award in Ghana)
- Recipient of the 2020 Outstanding Achievement Award in the Westminster Alumni Award of the University of Westminster, London, U.K.
- Named as a Young Global Leader of the World Economic Forum.
- Attended the Blavatnik School of Government, University of Oxford, Oxford, U.K. and completed an Executive Education Programme called Rising Public Leaders Programme.
- Qualified as an Insolvency Practitioner and member of the Chartered Institute of Restructuring and Insolvency Practitioners.
- Appointed a Notary Public of the Supreme Court of Ghana.
- Appointed Vice President of the Association of European Attorneys and African Vice President of

- the International Committee of the Arbitration Court of the Associations of European Attorneys.
- Appointed as a Conciliator on the Panel of Conciliator and an Arbitrator on the Panel of Arbitrators of the International Centre for the Settlement of Investment Disputes of the World Bank Group.
- Appointed to act as Secretary to the President of Ghana, Nana Addo Dankwa Akufo-Addo.
- Recipient of the National Honour, Grand Medal of Ghana.
- Attended and completed an Executive Education Programme on Global Leadership and Public Policy for the 21st Century at the Harvard Kennedy School, Cambridge, Massachusetts, U.S.A.

# ABOUT THE AUTHOR

Kow Abaka Essuman is the former Legal Counsel to the President of the Republic of Ghana, who also served as Acting Secretary to the President during the last four months of the President's term. He is a lawyer by profession, qualified to practise law in three jurisdictions: England and Wales, New York State, and Ghana. In 2022, he was sworn into office as a Notary Public of the Supreme Court of Ghana by the Chief Justice of Ghana. He is the Chairman and Senior Consultant for a boutique law firm in Accra, VINT and Aletheia PRUC, with an office in New York, U.S.A. He is a certified Insolvency Practitioner and a member of the Ghana Association for Restructuring and Insolvency Advisors. He currently serves as the Vice President of the Association of European Attorneys (AEA) and the African Vice President on the International Committee of the Arbitration Court of the AEA.

Before entering public service, Kow practised law at Ghana's largest and top law firm, Bentsi-Enchill, Letsa, and Ankomah. Within four years of joining the firm, he was promoted to Senior Associate in the litigation and dispute resolution practice group.

During this time, he represented several leading corporate clients, including companies in mining, telecommunications, and real estate, as well as a billion-dollar hedge fund in New York in a case against Argentina.

In addition to his legal work, Kow has been involved in legal education, working with Web Legal Education and the New York Bar Company to prepare candidates for the New York Bar Exam. He also lectured on the law of Trusts as part of the University of London Bachelor of Laws (LL.B.) programme offered by Zenith University College in Accra. He served as a part-time lecturer at the Ghana School of Law, tutoring students in Advocacy and Professional Ethics. Kow is a former Associate Member of the Chartered Institute of Arbitrators in England and, from 2017 to 2023, acted as a Conciliator on the Panel of Conciliators for the International Centre for the Settlement of Investment Disputes of the World Bank (ICSID). He currently serves as an Arbitrator on the Panel of Arbitrators for ICSID. Kow was a Founding Board Member of the State Interests and Governance Authority and the Minerals Income Investment Fund, Ghana's sovereign wealth fund.

Kow has received several recognitions for his

contributions and accomplishments, including his selection as a Global Shaper of the World Economic Forum in 2013 and his role representing the Global Shapers Community as one of its 80 Members at the World Economic Forum on Africa in Cape Town, South Africa, in 2015. In May 2015, Kow was featured and described as "Internationally Known and Locally Accepted" in the Future of Ghana's 30 Under 30 Maiden Edition. In June 2015, he appeared on the front page of the widely read Business and Financial Times in an article titled "Smart Suits, Fine Legal Brains." He has also been featured on various radio and television shows, including Speak Up, an anti-corruption advocacy show on ETV Ghana, and Just The Law, which aimed to educate the public about legal matters on Viasat One.

Furthermore, in 2017, Kow was voted the Most Influential Young Ghanaian and was nominated as part of the Class of 2018 in the 100 Most Influential Young Persons of African Descent, under the auspices of the United Nations International Decade for People of African Descent. In December 2019, he was presented with an Honorary Award by the President of Ghana, who is also the Chief Patron of the Head of State Award Scheme, for his contributions and support towards the growth and development of young people in Ghana through the Award Scheme. In 2020, he received the Outstanding Achievement Award from the University of Westminster for his professional accomplishments. In September 2021, he was appointed to the New Voices Council of the Apolitical Foundation. In March 2023, Kow was named a Young Global Leader by the World Economic Forum.

Kow received his education at the University of Westminster and BPP Law School in London, as well as Cornell University in New York, where he obtained a Master of Laws (LL.M.) degree with Honors in International Mergers and Acquisitions and Financial Institutions. He also holds an Executive Education Certificate in Oil, Gas and Mining Governance from the Blavatnik School of Government at the University of Oxford, another Executive Education Certificate from the Rising Public Leaders Programme at the same school, an Executive Education Certificate in Negotiation and Leadership from Harvard Law School, and an Executive Education Certificate in Global Leadership and Public Policy for the 21st Century from the Harvard Kennedy School.

In 2024, the President of Ghana awarded Kow the National Honour known as the Grand Medal of Ghana for his exemplary service to the Republic. Kow is a Christian and a passionate advocate for Jesus Christ, dedicating time to spread the Gospel through his writings on social media, his blog, in the pulpit, and at Christian gatherings. He is married to his beautiful wife, Lady-Ann, and together, they have two children, Papa Kwesi Abaka and Ewuradwoa Okyerewa Krofa.